How to double your sales

How to double your sales

The ultimate Master Class in how to sell anything to anyone

Bruce King

**Financial Times
Prentice Hall
is an imprint of**

Harlow, England • London • New York • Boston • San Francisco • Toronto • Sydney • Toronto
Singapore • Hong Kong • Seoul • Taipei • New Delhi • Cape Town • Madrid • Mexico City
Amsterdam • Munich • Paris • Milan

PEARSON EDUCATION LIMITED

Edinburgh Gate
Harlow CM20 2JE
Tel: +44 (0)1279 623623
Fax: +44 (0)1279 431059
Website: www.pearsoned.co.uk

First published in Great Britain in 2010

ISBN: 978-0-273-73261-7

British Library Cataloguing-in-Publication Data
A catalogue record for this book is available from the British Library

Library of Congress Cataloging-in-Publication Data
A catalog record for this book is available from the Library of Congress

10 9 8 7 6 5 4 3 2 1
13 12 11 10

Typeset in 9/13pt ITC Stone Serif by 3
Printed and bound in Great Britain by Henry Ling Ltd, at the Dorset Press,
Dorchester, Dorset

The publisher's policy is to use paper manufactured from sustainable forests.

For my wife Stephanie, my daughters Gemma and
Natasha, my son-in-law Ari and my grandson Asher.
And for everyone in sales without whom
all commerce would cease.

More praise for
How to double your sales

'In *How to double your sales*, Bruce King gives the most practical and effective advice on how to boost sales quickly that I've read in years. Anyone and everyone in sales should own a copy.'

Ivan R Misner PhD, *New York Times* best selling author and founder of BNI

'This is the best book on selling I have ever read. So very inspiring! It's practical, easy to follow and I would be very surprised if you did not double your sales very fast indeed.'

Thomas Power, Chairman – Ecademy

'Bruce King really aggravates me because he delivers sales magic that really works and dares to call it common sense! You will want to implement all his strategies and he makes that process so easy. So treat yourself to a dollop of Bruce's common sense.'

John Donnelly, past Vice President of The Institute of Directors and author of *Weapons Grade Business Tools*

'Whether you are new to sales or an experienced sales professional, this book will become your personal tool to help you double your sales fast. Make sure everyone in your company gets a copy.'

Reg Athwal, leading authority on human capital management and author of *Wake Up And Live The Life You Love*

'A practical step-by-step approach that will surely improve your sales performance. This is not something to be kept and filed away but a tool to accompany increased success in sales and re-focus you time and time again.'

Andy Lopata, co-author of the Amazon best seller *And Death Came Third – The Definitive Guide to Networking*

'This is THE sales book for everyone and especially those who spend too much time looking outside of themselves and overlook their innate personal strengths! Especially good focus and practical tips on how to get that "inner sales knowledge" working and simple ways to follow through. Thank you Bruce for putting me back on track.'

Pauline Crawford, Managing Director, Corporate Heart, putting 'life' back into business – mapping professional behaviour to turbo-charge business back to life!

'This is a "must-have" business book for the sole trader, budding entrepreneur and serious salesperson. They will benefit greatly from understanding and applying its excellent methods and systems. Tried and tested, pragmatic and straightforward – the wisdom of years related to success for the modern day. Keep it away from your competitors.'

Steve McNulty, Chairman of 'The Board', the UK's Prestigious Executive Business Club

'Bruce King's well-researched book challenges your current mind-set on the fastest way to close that deal. His proven strategy and sales-efficient tactics show you how to make every day of the week a highly profitable one – for both your customers and yourself.'

Carole Spiers, international authority on Corporate Stress, BBC Broadcaster. Author of best-selling *Tolley's Managing Stress in the Workplace* and *Turn Your Passion into Profit*.

'Wow! Made me feel young and excited again and continuously reminded me why I love selling. Definitely worth reading and implementing the valuable lessons in *How to double your sales*.'

Abhi Naha, Vice President of Global Sales for Idem and Chairman of the Beatbullying Charity

'This book is both captivating and extremely rich! The author delivers on all levels. I highly recommend this to any sales executive looking for the edge!'

Craig Goldblatt, author of *The Oscar Principles*

'So much of selling is about how you approach the sale, and really understanding the impact that you are having. Bruce has managed to capture the essence of the best and provides it in an easy to understand clear text that inspires and motivates as you read. Bruce starts with the end in mind, fixes your sales time management and moves on to the other sales blockers we suffer from. Bruce ensures results from day one.'

William Buist, Chairman, Abelard Management Services

'As a professional business coach, I can assure you that there is no wasted real estate in Bruce King's latest book. It not only contains important sales tips and techniques, but it is like having your own personal coach standing over your shoulder!'

Frankie Picasso, author of *The Unstoppable Coach, turning Impossible Goals into Unstoppable Outcomes*

Contents

Foreword

Everyone in business is in sales. As a salesperson, you are selling your ideas, products and services to your customers or clients and to those in senior positions in your organisation. If you are a Sales Manager, you are selling to your team and to your customers and clients. As the Chairman, President, Chief Executive Officer or Managing Director, you are selling your company, your ideas, your products or services to your financiers, your shareholders, the press, your team and possibly your key customers and clients too. So selling is an essential business skill; but there are others too.

Over the past 30+ years, I have had the pleasure and privilege of working with people at every level within organisations. The one thing I have observed is that the most successful people have four key attributes which often overcome a lack of selling skills to some degree. Combine these attributes with superb selling skills and anyone can easily get to the very top of the sales profession. These attributes are vision, commitment, determination and persistence. Here is a true story about a gentleman called Albert Weinstock.

❝ the four key attributes are vision, commitment, determination and persistence ❞

I was first introduced to Albert when I was asked to present a series of Sales Master Classes to 25 of the top salespeople working within a large financial services organisation. These were the top 25 of 3000 financial services salespeople, so you can imagine they were very successful people already. Albert, however, stood out like a sore thumb. Whilst the other 24 salespeople were extremely well dressed, looked very fit and were very articulate, the politest thing I can say about Albert was that he was the complete opposite of that. Nevertheless, based on his sales record, Albert had earned his place in the top 25.

When I asked the salespeople how they would explain in 15 seconds what they did for their clients, they had some very interesting and sophisticated ways of describing themselves. One example was: 'I help people minimise the effects of taxation during their lifetimes and ensure that as much of their estate as possible is passed on to their families on their death rather than into the government coffers.' Another was: 'I help people to plan their financial affairs so that they are able to retire 10 years earlier than they would otherwise be able to do so.' In total contrast was Albert's. He said: 'I sell life insurance, pensions and savings plans.'

I was fascinated by Albert and in one of the coffee breaks I sat down with him to find out more. It transpired that Albert had worked in the postal services, delivering mail for many years, until his mother became widowed and quite ill and he was unable to care for her properly on his postman's salary. He had applied for several other jobs without success when he heard that very good incomes could be made in financial services, and as it was commission only based, they were not too fussy who they took on. He told me that after the interview when he was offered a position, and found out what he could earn if he was successful, he became absolutely committed and determined to succeed in his new career. He had a vision of what he could achieve. He sold his car and everything else he thought he could do without and raised enough money to be able to keep himself and his mother for six months whilst he was learning his new trade.

❝ the salesman had a vision of what he could achieve ❞

Albert tried many of the sophisticated approaches used by the top salespeople in his company but was not comfortable with them, and he failed dismally. Then he decided to try a totally different approach; one that he himself invented. This approach quickly earned him the nickname 'Tower Block Albert'. This is what he did.

Albert took a bus or train to the nearest tower block of apartments. He would take the elevator to the top floor and then walk down and ring the bell on every front door. If it was answered he would say: 'Good afternoon Sir (or Madam). My name is Albert Weinstock, representing the (XYZ) Company. I sell life insurance, pensions and investment plans. I am here today introducing myself and making appointments for next Wednesday with people who would like to buy one or other of those. Would you like to make an appointment with me too?'

I have to say that I cringed at this approach, but the fact is that by the time Albert had reached the ground floor he had always made at least four appointments, and when he went back, he sold to every single one of them. He had, after all, pre-closed them. That was Albert's sole method of prospecting for new customers. He did this day after day, week after week and month after month. I consider that to be one of the most extraordinary examples of vision, commitment, determination and persistence, and a lesson for us all.

Think back to any time in your life when you had a vision and were absolutely, totally committed to achieve something. I know you achieved it because a vision and an absolute commitment to achieve it is incompatible with failure.

Think back to any time in your life when you were absolutely determined to achieve something. I know you achieved it because absolute determination is incompatible with failure.

Think back to any time in your life when you persistently worked towards achieving something. I know you achieved it because persistence is absolutely incompatible with failure.

If you follow everything I have to share with you in this series of Master Classes and are committed, determined and persistent in applying these techniques, you cannot fail to double your sales – fast!

Preface

This book represents a radical deviation from the style and content of most books that claim to improve your sales performance. The reason it is so different is because it is a lot more than just about selling techniques. In order for you to understand this difference and why it is so important, it may help to know a little more about my background.

I am most well known for my work in sales. What most people do not know is what I was doing with my life prior to joining the sales profession. Shortly after I left college I became very involved in the field of complementary medicine. It was called alternative medicine in those days. I studied nutrition, acupuncture and various other alternative medical practices. I worked with homoeopaths, osteopaths, psychologists and people from various other alternative medical disciplines as well as some traditional medical practitioners who were open minded to the alternative approaches. One of the subjects that I spent a lot of my time investigating and working on with my clients was how to use the power of the mind to help people heal themselves, a series of techniques similar in many ways to neuro linguistic programming (NLP).

On the face of it, my career in 'alternative' medicine was very successful. I had my own radio programme on Radio London, I wrote for several magazines and I ran an alternative medical centre in London which was one of the first in the UK. But the truth of the matter is that alternative medicine was not as popular in those days as it is now and I found it hard to make a decent living. With an expanding family and the associated expenses, and after some considerable soul searching, I decided to leave the field of alternative medicine and find a more financially rewarding career. A few months later, and by a bizarre series of coincidences, I found myself working in sales.

I became very successful, very quickly and I was a top sales performer with several companies. In the following years, I went on to build and train sales teams for other companies and I was even more successful. Then I set up my own business in financial services and built a sales team for my company. At one time I was employing and managing a team of over 70 salespeople, most of whom were selling at least twice the industry average.

The reason I was so successful in sales and the reason I was so successful coaching other salespeople was that I used the same mind control techniques I had used to help people heal themselves to help others become more successful in business and in sales.

You have almost certainly heard the expression 'it's all in the mind'. That is a lot closer to the truth than many people believe. You've possibly also heard the quote: 'There are two types of people in this world; those who think they can and those who think they cannot. And they are both right!' So in order to achieve a dramatic increase in sales, fast, we have to train our brains to believe we can, and we shall be working on that in the first Master Class. Here is an example to illustrate that point.

❝ we have to train our brains to believe we *can* ❞

Richard is a top salesman with a large manufacturer of agricultural machinery. He attended my Master Class because, in his own words, 'I want to be even better than I am now.' During one of the breaks he told me how his business had failed, how he had been on the point of giving up on life and how, 10 years previously, in a last desperate effort, he had applied for a sales job with an office equipment company.

As with so many people when they are first recruited into the sales profession, his prospective employer had sold him the job. Let's face it, when a company pays a very low salary, if any at all, and when your income is dependent on you getting out there and selling, they don't have a great deal to lose if they make the wrong choice. Richard was told that the job was easy, that he would make a fortune, that anyone could do it and that little training was necessary. He took the job and, after three days learning about the products he was to sell and the company's systems, off he went into the big wide world. All the enthusiasm engendered during those first few days rubbed off on him. Psychology in practice! After the first week on the road he returned to the office with a bundle of order forms for various items of equipment. He felt good about himself for the first time in ages. Life was good again – or was it? Back at the office he met some of his sales colleagues and that was when psychology turned against him:

- 'You've been lucky this week', one said.
- 'Your first week is always good and after that it's downhill all the way', another said.
- 'The competition's too stiff', remarked a third.

Guess what? Correct. At the end of the second week he had not sold anything.

Fortunately for Richard, he never forgot the excitement of that first week, or the money he had made. He vowed to make a success of himself. He improved his knowledge of his product range, went to various sales training courses to polish his sales techniques and studied avidly. He has never looked back. Yet that non-positive encounter with the effects of psychology could have ended his sales career after just one week.

I have also always been fascinated by the mental processes involved when people communicate with each other and how they make decisions. When I first embarked on my selling career I set out to investigate these processes and ensure I could communicate most effectively with people and speak with them in a way that would positively influence their decisions. My own studies in this field were dramatically enhanced when neuro linguistic programming (NLP) was developed and I combined many of those techniques with my own; these I will share with you in some of the following Master Classes.

Before I go on to explain how to use this book let me emphasise that, although I am going to teach you techniques which will increase your sales dramatically, these are not a substitute for a poor technical knowledge of your product or service. If you don't know enough about what you are trying to sell, you had better find out fast.

> **sales techniques are not a substitute for a poor technical knowledge**

I have often heard sales managers tell their salespeople that technical knowledge is not important; that as long as they know 5 per cent more than the person they are selling to they will appear to be experts. Make no mistake about that statement – it is rubbish! If you really want the fortune that being a top salesperson can bring, it is essential to know the technical aspects of the product or service you are selling. Why? First of all, and particularly due to the amount of information freely available on the internet, the average customer is a lot more informed than he or she might have been some years ago. They are looking for expert and trusted advice and in this highly competitive world it is readily available to them. If you do not know everything you should know about what you are selling, how can you possibly expect anyone to buy it?

It is also important to understand that it is very rare nowadays for anyone to have a completely unique product or service. If you take what you are currently selling and compare it with your competitor's product or service, you will most likely find that what you may have considered to be your unique selling proposition (USP) is in fact of little or no difference from your competitors'. So in most cases, you have only one USP – and that is YOU!

Finally, let me start these Master Classes with what I hope to be a thought-provoking statement:

Selling is not something you do TO somebody; it is something you do FOR somebody.

You therefore owe it to yourself and your customers to be the best you can be, and these Master Classes will coach you to be the very best.

How to use this book

It is a mistake to look too far ahead. Only one link in the chain of destiny can be handled at a time.
Winston Churchill

In an ideal world, I would like to have been able to publish this book as 10 separate books. You would have paid for all 10 in advance and been given the Foreword, Preface, Instructions and Master Class 1 when you made the purchase. You would have been instructed to concentrate on learning and applying what was taught in that first Master Class for one week before receiving the next Master Class in the post, and thereafter you would have been sent the subsequent Master Classes at weekly intervals. We do not however live in a perfect world, and even if we could have adopted that approach, the purchase price would have had to be considerably higher and possibly prohibitive for many people.

I am also not naive enough to think that if I ask you to study only one Master Class at a time and apply what you learn in each Master Class for at least one week before reading on, that you would resist the temptation to read the entire book right the way through. If you can, that would be terrific. If you really cannot, here is what I would like you to do instead.

Having read the entire book and picked out a few techniques that immediately captivate you that you want to put into practice right away, go back to the beginning and start again. Your curiosity will have been satisfied and so, this time, you can study each Master Class diligently and persistently apply those tech-niques you learn for one week before moving on to the next Master Class. In some instances you may want to take a little longer to become expert at a particular skill, in which case, do not move on to the next Master Class until you are ready to do so. Participate in these Master Classes this way and within a week your sales will be on the increase and that increase will gain momentum as you work your way through the series of 10.

A word of caution...

Another expression you have probably heard is 'If you carry on doing things the way you have always done them, the best you can expect are the same results.' Albert Einstein said that the definition of madness was doing things the way you have always done them and expecting different results.

If you want to double your sales – fast, it's quite obvious that you are going to have to do some things differently. There, for many people, is the challenge, because I am going to ask you to do various things that you may not be used to doing and which, at first, may make you feel a little uncomfortable. To illustrate my point, do the following exercise now:

- Put your hands in front of you and interlock your fingers and thumbs.
- Now take them apart and, this time, interlock them so that the other thumb is on top.
- How does that feel now? Does it feel different? 'Uncomfortable' is how most people describe the feeling when we do this exercise at one of my workshops. But do it often enough and it soon starts to feel comfortable.

If you really want to double your sales – fast, you are going to have to step out of your comfort zone and start doing the things I teach you in order to help you get to where we both want you to be.

Publisher's acknowledgments

The publishers are grateful to Stephanie Gee, Marie Scarves, for permission to reproduce the letter on page 16.

Train your brain to win the game
The game being to double your sales – fast!

Whatever the mind can conceive and believe, the mind can achieve.
Napoleon Hill, author of *Think and Grow Rich*

How the human brain works

One of the first things you have to do in order to double your sales fast, or indeed achieve anything you want in life very quickly, is to train your brain to believe you can, and to train it to help you to achieve that. So let us first of all take a look at how the human brain works.

The human brain is incredibly complicated. It's made up of at least 100 billion neurones, which is the technical name for nerve cells. To get that into perspective, there are approximately 100 billion stars in our galaxy. You have as many brain cells in your head as there are stars in our galaxy!

There are only 8 billion people living on earth. You have 14 times more brain cells in your head than there are people on planet earth!

I explained this to my eight-year-old niece a little while ago. Her response was, 'Do we really use all of those brain cells Bruce?', to which my reply was that I suspected most of us had a lot of spare capacity.

For the sake of simplicity, I like to compare the human brain to a computer. Firstly we have the conscious mind. I liken that to the

screen on your computer. It is what you are conscious of at any
given time. It is the words and sounds you are conscious of
hearing and the words you say to yourself when you are
thinking. It is what you are looking at and the pictures you create
in your mind when you are thinking and when other people are
speaking to you. The conscious mind deals with what you are
consciously aware of at the time and it can only handle a limited
amount of information at any one time. The conscious mind will
deal with the task you are focused on at the time.

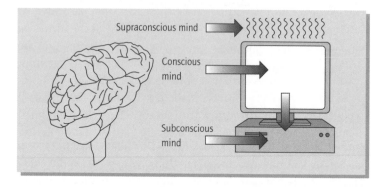

Then we have the subconscious mind, which I liken to the hard
drive on your computer. Everything that ever appears on your
computer screen or in the conscious mind is stored in the subconscious mind, or hard drive. Everything from the day you were
born. Some experts say that this even happens whilst you are still
in your mother's womb. The only difference between your brain
and the computer is that you do not need to press a 'save' button
for it to be stored; it happens automatically and is out of your
control.

Day by day, month by month and year by year, everything you
experience in your conscious mind is stored in your subconscious
mind and, over time, we build up automatic connections
between the conscious and the subconscious mind. Scientists call
these neuronal pathways. In this way, whenever your conscious
mind perceives anything, it automatically links to a previous
experience stored in your subconscious mind that relates to that
particular item of information. According to Professor Chris

Frith, one of the world's most renowned experts on the human brain, 'free will is illusory in that before we consciously decide to do anything, our subconscious mind has already made the decision on what we are going to do'. In fact 99.99 per cent of everything we do and think happens on a subconscious level. (In other words – we are all programmed rather like computers!) It is also one of the reasons why so many people continue to make the same mistakes over and over again whilst others achieve one success after another.

The major ways in which we create these neuronal pathways, or automatic links, are through the words we hear and the words we say, through the pictures we see around us and the pictures we create in our minds, the combination of which create feelings. The problem we have is that, according to behavioural psychologists, for every one positive experience, we have 480 negative experiences. In other words, we are subconsciously programmed to fail. Because we are programmed to fail, I know that no matter how successful you have been in the past, you have probably not even scratched the surface of what you are really capable of and why I know the techniques I am going to share with you can help you achieve so much. Let us take a look at how some of this negative programming takes place.

There is very little good news in the newspapers, in magazines, on the radio or television. Good news doesn't sell, so we are constantly bombarded with negative, or what I prefer to call 'non-positive', messages, which are all stored in the subconscious mind.

Did you ever have the words 'must try harder' written on any of your school reports? If you did, then you associate the word 'try' with failure. So later in life when somebody says they will 'try' to do something for you, you don't really expect them to do it. Neither does your subconscious mind help you when you say you will try to do something. Most times you do not.

❝ have you ever experienced a 'strong gut feeling'? ❞

Have you ever experienced a 'strong gut feeling' about any situation? Of course you have. That is the subconscious mind sending you a message.

There is one more part to the brain that you need to be aware of, which is the supraconscious mind. I liken this to the radiation coming off your computer. More on the supraconscious mind follows later in this Master Class.

Let us now take a closer look at how negative messages can affect your subconscious mind, your mental state and sales performance.

When you first picked up this book you may have thought that it was not really possible to double your sales fast, but if you could just get a 10 to 15 per cent increase in sales over a reasonable period of time you would be happy. If so, what you did was simply programme your subconscious mind to restrict your increase in sales to 10 to 15 per cent.

You may have thought that you would nevertheless 'try' to double your sales. I have already mentioned the word 'try' and its negative connotation. If you try to double your sales, you will almost certainly fail to do so.

When somebody telephones you and says 'I'm sorry to bother you but…', how do you feel? It is likely you will be less than enthusiastic to have a conversation with them. The words 'I'm sorry' connect to experiences in your subconscious mind when somebody had done something wrong. The word 'bother' is subconsciously associated with somebody being a nuisance. Then they say 'but', which means in spite of the fact that they know they are doing something wrong and are going to be a nuisance, they are going to do it anyway! Do you use that expression sometimes?

How many times have you heard or said the words 'no problem' when somebody has requested something. Think about the word 'problem' and what it could be associated with in somebody's subconscious mind. Why would anyone ever want to leave you, or you want to leave anyone, thinking about a problem?

How about 'Don't hesitate to call me'? What is the word 'hesitate' going to connect to or implant in the subconscious mind? Hesitation of course!

Have you ever said to anyone, 'Would you object to me calling you tomorrow?' When you ask that, they automatically have a subconscious 'objection' to what you have suggested. So the words you speak and the words you hear can have a dramatic and non-positive effect on your and other people's conscious and subconscious mind.

How about the pictures we see around us and the pictures we create in our minds when we are thinking about something? The following is a demonstration I have carried out hundreds of times at conferences around the world. You can do this yourself now or sometime later, and you need somebody to help you.

Stand up straight and hold your strongest arm straight out in front of you with the palm of your hand facing down. Ask the person helping you to put their hand over your extended wrist and press down very firmly. At the same time you must resist their downward pressure on your arm with all your strength. Just one word of caution – this is not a competition to see who is strongest. You are just working together to see how strong your arm feels. When you do this, you will be able to resist the downward pressure quite easily.

Now repeat the exercise but this time whilst you are looking at the picture below. This is a cartoon of a salesperson whose sales have fallen dramatically and they do not know what to do about it. I call him 'Mr Negative'.

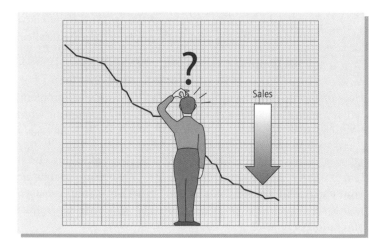

I guarantee your arm was a lot weaker this time! The negative picture you were looking at connected with other negative situations in your subconscious mind and your body became weaker as a result. The negative or non-positive pictures we see around us and in our minds can have an extraordinarily powerful non-positive effect on our entire state. As I said previously, words and pictures create feelings and if we hear non-positive words or see non-positive pictures, we feel non-positive at a subconscious level, which of course affects our conscious mind too.

I said earlier that the conscious mind can only handle small chunks of information at a time and it is therefore fairly obvious that if we were to attempt to stay consciously focused all day long on our major goal, we would not have time to deal with anything else. We therefore need to programme the subconscious mind to achieve our goals and the part of the brain we want to activate is called the reticular activating system (RAS).

Once the RAS has been programmed to know precisely what goals you want to achieve, it will do two things for you. Firstly, it will make you aware of opportunities around you and attract opportunities to you that can help you to achieve your goals. Secondly, it will filter all the information coming in to you from your environment and from your subconscious mind and only allow in the information you need to achieve your goals.

Here is a practical demonstration of how the RAS functions. In a moment, and wherever you are right now, stop reading and look around you. For just one minute I would like you to see how many items you can spot that are coloured green. Do that now.

I'm sure you saw many. But how many items did you observe that were coloured red? I doubt you saw any. What you did was to consciously programme the RAS to seek out items coloured green and by doing so, it filtered out just about anything else it had not been programmed to look for. When you programme your RAS consciously and subconsciously to seek out information for you that will help you to achieve any goal, that is precisely what it will do.

In the next section I am going to teach you several techniques and exercises that will help you to subconsciously programme your RAS to enable you to double your sales – fast. I call this process the GAVA process. GAVA stands for goals, affirmations, visualisation and action. I developed the GAVA process many years ago, before neuro linguistic programming (NLP) began to emerge as a science in its own right and became so popular. If you are familiar with NLP, you will see that there are some distinct similarities.

Now here is the most important point for you to understand. I told you earlier that our brains were a little like computers and that you were programmed rather like the hard drive. So here is the key point:

> You do not need to believe these techniques will work for them to work for you. They will – whether you believe it or not! You just have to use them. You have been programmed randomly most of the time in the past and now it is time to apply some planned programming to help you to double your sales – fast!

I have taught many thousands of people the following techniques and almost without exception, they have gone on to achieve a great deal more than they ever believed was possible. Use them every day and within a remarkably short space of time, sometimes in just a few hours and certainly within a few days, I guarantee you will start to see some quite extraordinary changes in your attitude, your energy levels, your confidence and, of course, your sales.

The GAVA double your sales – fast process

The G in the GAVA process – Goals

I am sure you know how important goal setting is. Some expressions that relate to it and spring to mind are:

■ If you don't know where you are going, how will you ever know when you get there?

- A person without goals is like a ship without a rudder. You just get blown about by the winds and tides of life.
- We all have two choices: we can make a living or design a life.

One of the most powerful things that someone once said to me which had the biggest impact on my life was: 'Bruce, you have two choices in life: You can be an extra in somebody else's production or the star of your own. Without clearly defined goals you'll just be someone else's extra!'

From the point of view of what we are doing together now, there is only one goal! I want you to double your sales – fast – and you presumably also want to. Enough said! So here is how you programme your RAS to help you achieve just that.

To prepare yourself for implementing the GAVA process and some of the exercises that follow, it is important to understand that just having a simple stated goal such as 'double my sales' is not sufficient. You must also set a date by which you will achieve the goal because a goal without a deadline is nothing more than a dream, or possibly even a delusion. Goals must have a specific deadline in order to be achieved.

Your RAS will also work far more effectively and faster when it knows in as much detail as possible what your lifestyle will be and how you will feel when you have achieved that goal. The clearer the picture, the more accurately it can focus and target your goals. In order to prepare for this I would like you to take half an hour, or possibly more if you need it, and complete the following written exercise. As with other written exercises I will be asking you to do during these Master Classes, you may find it better to complete the exercise on a separate sheet of paper and then transfer your answers into this book when you are satisfied with your final version.

❝ the clearer the picture, the more accurate the focus and target of your goals ❞

For this first exercise (Exercise 1.1 – overleaf), I would like you to imagine how your life will be when you have doubled your sales by the specified date. If doubling your sales will enable you to purchase a prestigious new car, be given a larger office, have savings set aside, buy a new home and take a luxury holiday, and that is what you would do, then write all this down in as much detail as possible.

If you want to own a new sports car, be specific. Write down the make, the colour of the paintwork and the upholstery. If you would have a larger office, describe it in detail. If you will gain accumulated savings – write down the amount. If it is a new house, the same applies. You need to know where that house would be, the colour of the brickwork, the window-frames and the roof. You need to know the style of the property and the number of rooms. If it is a luxury holiday, where will you be going, who will you be going with and where will you be staying? The more detail you can write down, the more likely you are to achieve it.

Do Exercise 1.1 now or as soon as you are able to. Then follow on with Exercises 1.2 to 1.4 on the following pages.

exercise 1.1

Imagine ...

What my life will be like when I have doubled my sales by _____ (date):

_____

_____

_____

_____

_____

_____

_____

_____

_____

_____

_____

_____

_____

_____

_____

_____

_____

_____

_____

_____

_____

_____

_____

_____

If you prefer not to write in this book, this form and all others are
available to download at www.bruceking.co.uk/doubleyoursales

Post your goal to double your sales

Purchase a pad of yellow adhesive notes and write on them as in the following illustration:

> I (your name)
> will double my
> sales by
> (date)

Write out about 15 of these notes and place them where you will come across them frequently during the course of the day. For example: on the corner of your computer screen, on the wall by your desk, on the dashboard or windscreen of your car, on your bathroom mirror, on the refrigerator door and anywhere else where you will see them often. You do not have to read the words every time you see them. Your subconscious mind will automatically recognise the words and continuously reinforce that message. You will be programming your RAS and your subconscious mind to double your sales by that date.

Keep a goal book

I would like you to purchase a smart leather or vinyl bound book with numerous blank sheets into which you can paste pictures. Write your goal on the first page in large, bold letters. Starting today, and over the next few weeks, collect and paste in pictures of the things you associate with having already achieved your goals. These could be pictures of your new car, your new office, your new house or your holiday in Barbados. Whatever pictures you come across that excite you and represent what your life will be like when you have doubled your sales, cut them out and paste them in. Keep your goal book with you at all times and look through it at least once a day.

Some of the people who have attended my Master Classes put a great deal of their success down to keeping a goal book. Some have said it was the most important factor in helping to keep them focused on doubling their sales.

exercise 1.4

Keep a daily journal

Buy a modest size diary with a page for each day, for the purpose of keeping a journal. At the end of every day, spend just 5–10 minutes writing down all the good things that have happened to you in the day that have moved you closer towards achieving your goals.

Also write down the things you have thought about that day, ideas that have 'popped into your mind' that you believe will also help you to achieve your goal of doubling your sales. When you have finished doing these written exercises, read what you have written and congratulate yourself for your achievements to date and on what you are going to do in the future.

The first A in the GAVA process – Affirmation

An affirmation is a scientifically proven form of auto-suggestion. It is a statement that you repeat over and over to yourself and is a promise to yourself that you will achieve a specific objective. In this case the objective is to double your sales by a specified date and this is the paragraph I want you to write down and learn:

I (your name) am committed to doubling my sales by (date) and they are already increasing rapidly. Nothing will stand in the way of me making (£X) in personal income this year.

Insert your name and the date by which you intend to have doubled your sales. Calculate the income you will make when you have doubled your sales and insert that figure, and then learn the affirmation off by heart. Say it aloud and with feeling 25 times, at least twice a day. You can do this whilst having a shower, walking in the park, jogging, in the car and any other time it is convenient for you to do so. The more times you say it every day, the faster you will programme your subconscious mind to help you achieve your goal to double your sales. If the situation you are in at the time precludes you from saying it out aloud, say it silently to yourself and with feeling.

The V in the GAVA process – Visualisation

This technique is, without question, the most powerful of them all. Some years ago I was involved in teaching people to walk barefoot across beds of burning hot coals. The reason for these fire-walking seminars was to demonstrate that it is possible to achieve the seemingly impossible in a very short period of time. The training consisted of a short period of relaxation, followed by 20 minutes of visualising walking across the red hot coals. More than 50 people were taught this simple technique at each one of our fire-walking seminars and at the end of the training very few lacked the confidence to walk across the burning coals. With few exceptions, there was not a blister in sight. Visualisation is the key to programming the subconscious mind, and one of the keys to helping you double your sales. Because it is so important, I am going to explain in more detail why this is such a powerful technique.

ff visualisation is the key to programming the subconscious mind jj

When you put an absolutely clear picture into your subconscious mind there are two main effects. Firstly, the effect this has on you and secondly, the effect it has on others.

The effect visualisation has on *you*

The first effect visualisation will have on you is based on the fact that the RAS cannot tell the difference between imagination and reality. Here are some examples to illustrate this very important point.

In a moment I want you to close your eyes and picture a lemon on a chopping board. Then see yourself cutting the lemon in half with a very sharp knife, revealing the shiny inside of the lemon and seeing the juice running down the side of the knife blade. Then picture yourself cutting a thin slice of the lemon, putting it inside your mouth and sucking it. Do that now.

Did you experience a strange feeling in your mouth just as you would have if you had actually been sucking on a piece of lemon?

I'm sure you did experience that sensation – but you were only imagining the lemon. Sometimes, the mind simply cannot tell the difference between imagination and reality.

Major James Nesbeth spent seven years as a prisoner of war in Vietnam. During those seven years he was imprisoned in a cage that measured only four and a half feet high by four feet wide and four feet long. Throughout almost the entire time he was a prisoner he saw no one, talked to no one and had no physical activity. In order to keep his sanity and his mind active, he described, during a TV interview, how he used visualisation techniques.

Every day, in his mind, he would play a game of golf – a full 18-hole game at his favourite golf course. In his mind, he would create pictures of the trees on the course, he would see and smell the freshly mown grass, hear and feel the wind and hear the songs of the birds. He created different weather conditions – windy spring days, overcast winter days and sunny summer mornings. He felt the grip of the club in his hands as he played his shots in his mind. He watched the ball arc down the fairway and land at the exact spot he had selected. He did this in his mind, seven days a week for seven years. He took as long playing this round of golf in his mind as if he were actually playing the course.

When Major Nesbeth was finally released and had the opportunity to play his first round of golf on that favourite golf course, he found that he had cut 20 strokes off his golfing average without having touched a golf club in seven years – just by practising in his mind. A further example demonstrating that the mind cannot tell the difference between imagination and reality.

An experiment was carried out with a group of basketball players in the USA. Thirty professional players were brought in and tested on their ability to take penalty shots. Once their standards were assessed they were split into three groups of 10. The first group was sent home and told to just rest up and forget about basketball for a week. The second group was brought in daily for seven days and made to practise taking penalty shots for one hour a day. The third group was instructed to stay at home, sit down in a chair, close their eyes and practise taking penalty shots in their mind for half an hour a day and to see themselves getting a 100 per cent score rate.

At the end of the week the three groups were brought back in and retested. The group that had done nothing remained at the same standard. The group that had come back and physically practised every day improved their performance by 5 per cent. The group that had practised in their minds every day improved by a staggering 14 per cent. Again, illustrating that the mind cannot tell the difference between imagination and reality.

That is the powerful effect that using visualisation can have on you. It trains your brain to achieve what you want to achieve, with considerably less effort and almost as if by magic.

The effect visualisation has on *others*

When I first start to discuss this topic at my conferences and workshops, approximately 50 per cent of the audience are quite sceptical. Those sceptics who put into practice what I am about to share with you are convinced in a very short while after doing so, and I can assure you there is a large body of scientific evidence to support these theories. However, I do not have the scope within this book to give you a grounding in quantum physics and the associated subjects that underpin these theories; so I shall keep the explanation quite simple.

Scientists have proved that if you take the smallest particles found on our planet such as protons, and you destroy these by smashing them into one another in a particle accelerator, all that is left is pure energy. It is believed by many of these scientists that energy is the underlying substance on which everything in the universe is based.

I, and millions of others around the world, are convinced that every human being is in some way connected to every other human being through an energy based network of interconnected information pathways. An analogy could be the internet.

Here are two examples which you can probably relate to a lot more easily and which should help to convince you of this concept.

You have been driving along in your car, in that way we sometimes do when we are almost on autopilot, or you have been sitting quietly in your office with your mind drifting. Suddenly somebody's face or name just pops into your mind. Have you ever, within a short while of that happening, received a telephone call from that very person and said, 'That's funny – I was just thinking about you', or you telephone them and they say the same thing? I know you have.

When I ask an audience of a thousand people that question, almost every hand goes up. When I then ask them if it has happened several times, every hand that went up the first time goes up again. This is not coincidence. This is you, or they, communicating thoughts and attracting people via these energy fields.

A little while ago I received a letter from a saleswoman working in wholesale fashion. She wrote the following:

Dear Bruce

I attended your Sales Master Class. I was highly sceptical about the visualisation exercises but as everything else you taught us made so much sense, I thought I'd at least give it a try.

Our business is wholesaling fashion accessories to stores. There are two major stores we have always wanted to supply but have never been able to get an appointment with the buyer. So I visualised them calling me and asking to see our latest range. I never believed they would and so was simply amazed when one of them called me on Wednesday morning and invited me in to meet them. And I was completely blown away when the second one called me on Friday afternoon!

I am just so excited and really into the visualisation exercise now. I will do this every day – forever.

Thank you so much!

Best wishes, Stephanie Gee – Marie Scarves

The fact is that we are all connected in some way and any thought by any human can be transmitted to anyone else in the species. The stronger the thought and the deeper in the subconscious – the stronger the energy's resonance and the more likely other people who can help you to achieve your goals are going to be attracted to you – the mind magnet!

exercise 1.5

Visualise your goal to double your sales

Carry out this exercise every day, twice a day. Find a quiet place where you are not going to be disturbed for 20 minutes. This could be a room in your home, a spare office at your place of work, or your car. I love carrying out these exercises in my car because I feel it is a very private space, almost like a cocoon, and I can park up anywhere where it is quiet, turn off my mobile and know I will not be disturbed.

Now I want you to close your eyes and, for just 3 minutes, relax and focus on breathing gently and listening to and feeling the breath going in and out of your body. You should feel very relaxed by the end of those 3 minutes.

Next, and for the following 17 minutes, I want you to visualise in as much detail as possible precisely how your life would be if you had already achieved your goal of doubling your sales. You take this information from the first written exercise you carried out earlier. I want you to see the pictures you associate with having doubled your sales. Those pictures might be you sitting in a much more prestigious car, or a larger office, seeing your bank statement with a very healthy balance on it, living in a new home, or sitting on a beach in Barbados. Whatever the pictures are that you associate with doubling your sales – see those pictures clearly and in the greatest of detail.

If, for example, you want to own a new sports car, you need to know the make, the colour of the paintwork and upholstery, the look of the dashboard, the colour and finish on the steering-wheel and the make of tyre. In other words, everything that would enable a stranger to produce a detailed picture of what is in your mind must be visualised.

If it is a new house, the same applies. You need to visualise the colour of the brickwork, the window-frames and the roof. You need to visualise the number of rooms and the décor in every one of those rooms, right down to the last detail. Most importantly, you need to visualise yourself living there, just as you need to imagine yourself owning and driving the sports car.

I also want you to hear the sounds associated with those pictures. It could be the sound of the exhaust or the engine of your new, prestige car. It could be the sound of people clapping and congratulating you on your large bonus and promotion. It could be the sound of the waves lapping the beach in Barbados. Whatever the sounds are that are associated with those pictures I want you to hear them.

Lastly, I want you to get in touch with your feelings. I want you to feel as you would feel if you had doubled your sales and were experiencing everything that went with that.

The first few times you carry out this exercise you may find that your mind tends to drift a little and you start thinking about other things. That is perfectly normal and nothing to be concerned about. As soon as you notice you have done this, just go back to the exercise. There is no need to make up for the time you lost when your mind drifted.

Your responsibility is to carry out these exercises every single day until you have achieved your goal. Most people tell me that they start to see quite extraordinary results within just a few days.

Very important note

In order to make this visualisation process easy for you to follow and even more effective in enabling you to achieve your goals, I have recorded a 20 minute audio track which talks you through the process over the relaxing background sound of waves breaking on the shoreline. It is free to download as an MP3 and is available at www.bruceking.co.uk/doubleyoursales

Now for a few more things I want you to do every day to ensure you achieve your goal to double your sales.

Change the words you use

From now on, I want you to be particularly conscious of the words you use when speaking to other people and the words you use in your mind when talking to yourself, and to change any non-positive words and phrases you use into positive ones. For example:

Instead of: It's not possible

Say: *It is possible*

Instead of: I'll try

Say: *I will.*

Instead of: I'm sorry to bother you but...

Say: *I have something to run past you which I'm sure you will be very excited about. Is now a good time to speak or please give me a specific time when I can call you back?*

Instead of: No problem.

Say: *It's a pleasure.*

Instead of: Would you object if I called you tomorrow?

Say: *May I call you tomorrow please?*

Listen very carefully to what you are saying to other people and, if you hear yourself saying anything with a non-positive connotation, correct yourself on the spot. Say something like – 'let me rephrase that'. When you are talking to yourself, do the same. From now on, it is time to start communicating with others and yourself in a totally positive way.

The following amusing story illustrates how non-positive thinking can create a non-positive result.

Mr Jones, a farmer, needed to plough his field before the dry spell set in, but his own plough had broken. 'I know, I'll ask my neighbour, farmer Smith, if I can borrow his plough. He's a good man; I'm sure he'll have done his ploughing by now and he'll be glad to lend me his machine.' So Mr Jones began to walk the four fields to Smith's farm.

After a field of walking, farmer Jones said to himself, 'I hope that farmer Smith has finished all his own ploughing or he'll not be able to lend me his machine.' Then after a few more minutes of worrying and walking, farmer Jones said to himself, 'What if Smith's plough is old and on its last legs – he'll never be wanting to lend it to me will he?'

After another field, farmer Jones said to himself, 'Farmer Smith was never a very helpful fellow, I reckon maybe he won't be too keen to lend me his plough even if it's in perfect working order and he's finished all his own ploughing weeks ago.'

As farmer Jones arrives at farmer Smith's farm, farmer Jones is thinking to himself: 'That old Smith can be a mean old fellow. I reckon even if he's got all his ploughing done, and his own machine is sitting there doing nothing, he'll not lend it to me just so he can watch me go to ruin.'

Farmer Jones then walked up farmer Smith's front path, knocked on the door, and farmer Smith answered. 'Well good morning Jones, what can I do for you?' said farmer Smith. Farmer Jones, with eyes bulging and a red face said, 'Mr Smith, you can take your bloody plough, and you can stick it up your back side!'

Avoid energy vampires

You are surrounded by non-positive people who are capable of sapping your positive energy. They will tell you that your goal to double your sales is crazy and impossible to achieve. They may laugh at your vision for success and be intent on bringing you down to their level. Do not let this happen. You will not be the first person to have doubled your sales using these techniques; thousands have gone before you.

If you had already achieved your goal of doubling your sales and living the lifestyle you want and deserve, would you be spending time with these people? Would you still be mixing in the same business and social circle? Possibly not. The time to make these changes is *now*. Act as if you are already the success you intend to

> **act as if you are already the success you intend to be**

be. Jim Rohn, the hugely successful author and self-made millionaire, put it most powerfully when he said: 'You are the average of the five people you spend the most time with!' I put it another way: 'If you want to be really successful in life and enjoy the benefits of that success, you need to fly with the eagles, not twitter with the sparrows.'

Change your employment status

If you are already running your own business then this does not apply to you. If you are employed it most certainly does. From now onwards I want you to think of yourself in a different way. Instead of thinking of yourself as an employee, I want you to think of yourself as the Chief Executive Officer of your own one-person corporation, currently selling your services to a particular person or company. That is the reality of your situation, so from now on act and behave like that CEO.

The last A in the GAVA process – Action

The action in this case is to put everything you have learned so far into practice and learn and implement the rest of the material in the following Master Classes. However, before we move on to the next Master Class I'd like to discuss with you some of the most common psychological barriers to success and if you are being held back by any of these, this is time to deal with them once and for ever.

Change is going on in the world all the time and so much of this change is out of our control. Most of the time we either have no choice but to go along with it and accept it. For example, there are cyclical changes in the stock market, changes in the weather in summer and winter, and changes in the value of house prices. These are beyond our direct control.

Then there are technological changes, such as the invention of the computer and the mobile telephone, to name but a few. You can choose to go along with these changes or reject them, but inevitably you will almost always accept them. I remember when computers first came to be used in business and my secretary swore she would never use one of those 'new fangled things'. She really did hang on in there but when we could no longer purchase typewriter ribbons she finally gave in and embraced the technology. I also remember when mobiles were first introduced and I was adamant I would never have one. Now of course I choose not to manage without it.

When it comes to changing yourself and your behaviours for the better, which is something entirely within your control, why then would you even think of resisting it? The answer is probably because you are scared – it is fear! Fear is the one feeling above all other emotions that holds people back from achieving the success they want and deserve, and is something you need to overcome if you are going to double your sales.

Are you fearful?

Some years ago, when I was working full time in sales, I was driving past a large office block which had the name 'Rogers & Associates – Accountants' on the face of the building in large letters. At the time, I was selling accounting systems for accountants and my first reaction was to stop and call in to introduce myself. Then fear set in. The little voice in my head was recalling past times when I had dropped in without an appointment and had been rejected, or had the opportunity to show them what I was selling and was told it was of no interest. I imagined how it would all be a waste of time. As a result of those thoughts, I kept driving. However, after a few hundred yards I put the brakes on my thoughts, turned the car around, drove back and dropped in. It transpired that the senior partner was an old college friend of mine. We had coffee, caught up on old times and, to cut a long story short, a few weeks later I received an order that earned me over £4000 in commission.

The truth of the matter is that most of the things we fear are just in our imagination. According to some psychologists 'fear' stands for Fantasised Experiences Appearing Real. In other words, the experiences we imagine may happen or they may not happen, but by imagining that they will, we create fear. If you don't believe me, take half an hour to list as many situations as you can think of when you were scared of what might happen if you did something – but you did it just the same. Then place a tick against those situations where what you feared would happen, did happen. I'm betting there are going to be very few ticks!

❝ today fear is a signal to us that we must be cautious ❞

Our stone age ancestors used fear as a way of dealing with dangerous situations. It was part of the 'fight or flight' mechanism that helped to keep them safe and the fear created an adrenaline rush that enabled them to deal with danger. Nowadays, we do not have to deal with the dangers that our ancestors experienced. Today fear is a signal to us that we must be cautious, alert and ready to deal with a specific situation, and we experience the same or a similar adrenaline rush. However, because we do not have to fight or fly, we transfer our fear into situations where we really need not be fearful at all. In spite of that, it is almost guaranteed you are going to experience fear frequently in your life. It is how you face up to it and how you deal with it that will make the difference between failure and success.

To help you understand how you manifest fear, look at the following statements.

- I am afraid of making a cold call.
- I am afraid of the sales presentation I have to make to a group of Directors.
- I am afraid of speaking with the Managing Director.

Now let us restate each of those in a different way.

- I want to be successful at cold calling but I get fearful by imagining I will be rejected and how I would feel.
- I want to make a good sales presentation to a group of Directors but I get fearful by imagining I will fail to make a really good impression.
- I want to speak with the Managing Director but I am fearful because I imagine he will not take me seriously as I am only a salesperson.

Do you see how you create the fear by imagining a non-positive outcome? Now ask yourself these questions.

- **Why should I fear rejection?** Rejection is nothing more than a myth because rejection never leaves me any worse off than before I was rejected.
- **Why should I fear failure?** It is perfectly OK to fail. As convenient as it might be, I cannot always learn from other people's mistakes. Sometimes I have to fail in order to learn how to do something better.
- **Why should I fear Managing Directors?** They are just people like me with their own families, their own goals, their own fears and, very often, are very fearful of salespeople too. As for fear of losing a sale; I have never yet met a salesperson who sold to every single person they ever wanted to sell to.

How we deal with fear is a choice

Sometimes we choose to face fear head on and we are exhilarated by it and love the experience. Other times we allow it to freeze us into inactivity.

Did you ever go on one of those really scary rollercoaster rides? You were possibly petrified when you were queuing for the ride – but you went anyway!

Do you snow ski? Do you ever get scared when approaching a new and slightly more dangerous run than you are used to? I know you do and I know that most times, if not always, you choose to ski it anyway. How you deal with fear is a choice. So why not always choose to be excited and exhilarated by it? Here is a technique you can use that will enable you to overcome fear and take positive action.

There will be many times in your life when you overcame a really powerful fear. It could have been the rollercoaster or skiing example I just mentioned. It could have been when you were learning to ride a two-wheeled bicycle and your parents took off the rear wheel stabilisers for the first time and said they would push you to get you started. You were possibly petrified and even fell off a few times. Every time you fell off, the fear became worse. Then finally you managed to keep your balance and pedalled off on your own. I know how fantastic you felt afterwards because the same thing happened to me.

Could it have been the first time you made a sales presentation to a board of Directors and walked away with the sale? Did you leave the office building, and once you were round the first corner, leap into the air and shout for joy?

Whatever that experience was when you overcame a powerful fear, I want you to sit quietly in a chair and use this NLP technique. Replay the whole scene through in your mind. See yourself doing what you did, hear the sounds associated with that experience, and feel all the power and excitement you felt when you beat it. At the moment you are feeling that power and excitement at its highest level, squeeze the lobe of your right ear between a finger and your thumb for a few seconds.

❝ replay the whole scene through in your mind ❞

Repeat this exercise several times and you will lock that feeling into your subconscious mind and associate it with squeezing your earlobe. Then, whenever you feel fear, squeeze your right earlobe and you will experience all the power and excitement you need to overcome that fear.

Fear is not something to be feared; it can be your greatest ally. Fear is a natural reaction and not something you should feel at all ashamed of admitting. Accept that being fearful is a natural stage in the process of achieving great success. Face the fear with courage and know that eventually, if you do this, you cannot fail to reach your goal of doubling your sales.

I'll be happy when...

If you are not happy right now, then it is very unlikely you are going to be happy when you have doubled your sales, and you are not going to be happy while you are on your way to achieving that goal. Unhappy people tend to be non-positive, less inclined

> **the word 'needy' is non-positive**

to action and often see the worst in every situation rather than the best. Unhappy people also tend to use the expression 'I need' rather than 'I want'. It's great to want more, but it is not OK to need more. Don't be needy! The word 'needy' is non-positive.

Unhappy people also attract other unhappy people to them, and the unhappy people you attract are going to be less likely to buy than happy ones. If you really want to double your sales, then I suggest you get happy right now. You already have many reasons to be so. For example, you may want a nicer home, but you do have a roof over your head right now and many people do not. You may want a more prestigious car, but you do have the two or four wheels you need to get around to see all those customers you are going to be selling to. You may want to be able to afford much more expensive designer clothes, but I am assuming you have some nice smart ones anyway. Are you getting the picture now?

If you are not really happy, here is an exercise that I would like you to do right now or at the earliest opportunity. It is one that I have people carry out in my Personal Growth Master Classes and it can really make you feel a lot happier than you have been for a very long time.

Complete Exercise 1.6 entitled *Reasons for me to be happy right now*. Take a close look at every area of your life; your work, your relationships, your home, your hobbies and everything else that comes to mind. Make a long list of everything you have got to be happy about in each of these areas. At the end of this long list you should write 'I'm also happy because I am now on my way to doubling my sales!'

When you have finished that list, read it again and keep this book with you at all times. Add to that list as you identify other things that make you happy. If necessary, staple an additional blank sheet on to it when you have run out of space. Any time you don't feel happy, take it out and read it again.

There is another advantage to being happy; happy people tend to smile a lot. People like people who smile and people buy from people they like.

exercise 1.6

Reasons for me to be happy right now

1 _____

2 _____

3 _____

4 _____

5 _____

6 _____

7 _____

8 _____

9 _____

10 _____

11 _____

12 _____

13 _____

14 _____

15 _____

16 _____

17 _____

18 _____

19 _____

20 _____

If you prefer not to write in this book, this form and all others are available to download at www.bruceking.co.uk/doubleyoursales

It's not my fault!

Do you make excuses for not achieving? Do you blame other people? Do you complain? If you do, it is time to stop right now. These habits create a motivational deficiency disorder. Everything you are experiencing in your life and work today are the result of choices *you* made in the past and it is time to start taking total responsibility for your life. Let us analyse these habits one at a time.

Do you make excuses?

If you do then it is going to be a lot harder for you to double your sales, or indeed achieve anything else you want in life. Excuses are a waste of time because no matter how many excuses you make, it will not change you and your situation at all. All it will do is create more non-positive neural pathways into your subconscious mind.

From now on you have to adopt the attitude 'If it is to be, it is up to me!' You have to come from a standpoint that you have always had the power to make a difference in your life but, until now, you have chosen not to use that power. It really does not matter if you chose not to in the past because the past is history and the only people who make money out of history are historians and archaeologists. It is time to change, stop making excuses and take total responsibility for your life. You can take as long over making this decision as you wish. You can think about it and drag it out over the next few weeks, or you can make the decision to take that responsibility right now. Your call!

In the future, when things don't go as well for you as you would have liked, and rest assured things will go wrong, instead of making excuses, ask yourself questions like:

- How did I create that situation?
- What did I say or not say that caused that non-positive result?
- What did I do to get that response?

- How can I make sure that does not happen in the future?
- What do I have to do differently to get the results I want?

Make it a lifelong mission to learn from your mistakes and from your successes and enjoy the experience.

Do you blame other people?

If you are going to double your sales, then you have to stop blaming other people for your lack of sales success. Blame is a waste of time because no matter how much you blame another person, it will not change you and your situation at all. Just like excuses, all it will do is create more non-positive neural pathways into your subconscious mind.

If something goes wrong, accept the blame and ask yourself the same questions to ensure it does not happen again. Of course there will be times when other people involved in the sales process or in the organisation make a mistake and, as a result, sabotage the sale. But, ultimately, people buy from people and it is up to you to overcome the situation. Nothing is insurmountable.

Stop complaining!

There are two aspects to complaining. The first is complaining about our current situation – and we can only do this when we know that something better already exists. Statements like:

- 'I don't have a big enough house'
- 'I don't have a smart enough car'
- 'I'm not earning enough money' or
- 'My sales manager is horrible to me'

are all complaints that you can do something about but have taken the decision not to. With this aspect of complaining, you simply need to stop and take total responsibility for your life.

There are also situations where you could have a legitimate complaint about something that is affecting your ability to double your sales as quickly as you wish, or could have resulted in you losing a sale through no fault of your own. Maybe the switchboard operator did not pass an important customer call on to you? Perhaps the order was not delivered on time? Maybe they sent the wrong size or the wrong colour? Things out of your control can and do go wrong and need dealing with, but in the correct manner.

Have you ever noticed that so many people who complain do so to the wrong people? A husband has an issue with his wife but complains to his friends at work about her. A mother has an issue with her children but complains to her mother. An employee has an issue with his boss but complains to workmates. Why do they do this? The answer is very simple. They complain to others because it is easier than complaining to the person they have the issue with. Of course, that rarely ever resolves the issue.

If you feel you have a reason to complain about something that is affecting your ability to double your sales, you need to deal with the issue with the person who caused the problem – but do not complain. The moment you tell someone you need to complain about something, or you act in a manner that is identified with complaining, their subconscious mind will switch them into a defensive mode and you will not get the level of cooperation you want in dealing with the situation. You may even alienate yourself from them and get even less cooperation in future.

ff deal with the person who caused the problem JJ

Instead, develop the habit of replacing complaining with asking for help and cooperation to ensure that the situation does not repeat itself. If the situation cannot be resolved, then go to a higher level, and if you are already making your point to the highest level of authority who cannot or will not help, then you may have to make the decision to sell your services to another organisation. Either way, things will then change. You have to create the situation and circumstances that will enable you to achieve your goals, not stand by and allow everything to happen to you.

That's all for this Master Class. From this point on, please study and work on applying the techniques you will learn in these Master Classes one week at a time. Take longer before moving on to the next one, if necessary.

Key action points

▪ Complete the written exercise *Imagine ... What my life will be like when I have doubled my sales.*

▪ Post your goal to double your sales.

▪ Keep a goal book.

▪ Keep a daily journal.

▪ Repeat your affirmation at least 25 times, twice daily, aloud and with feeling.

▪ Carry out the exercise *Visualise your goal to double your sales*, twice daily for 20 minutes, for at least the next six weeks.

▪ Change the words you use.

▪ Avoid energy vampires.

▪ Change your employment status.

▪ Get happy now – carry out the exercise *Reasons for me to be happy right now.*

▪ Make a commitment to stop making excuses and blaming other people. Take total responsibility for your life.

▪ Work with the *GAVA double your sales – fast* process every day and at least until you have completed all the Master Classes.

▪ Download your free MP3 visualisation audio at www.bruceking.co.uk/doubleyoursales.

2

Time management
Double your selling time and why people buy

Do not squander time for that is the stuff life is made of.
Benjamin Franklin, signatory to the US Declaration of Independence

Time management is obviously not specifically a sales technique. However, if you could get 50 per cent more selling time out of your working week, the chances are that you could double your sales just with good time management skills.

Time management techniques

There are numerous books you can read on the subject of time management and, whilst they all contain some excellent advice, some can tend to get rather complex. In fact, one person who recently came to a workshop of mine complained to me that after attending a time management course, he was so busy managing his time that he had far less time available than he had before he attended the course. Therefore, in this chapter I am going to share with you the three simple techniques that I use to manage my time and which are the most effective ones I know. Apply these diligently and you could easily double your selling time and double your sales – fast!

1 Do not waste your time

There are three ways you can use your time. You can waste it, spend it or invest it. The only sensible way is the last. One of the exercises I use at my conferences and workshops is to ask the audience to sit silently and watch the second hand of their wrist watch for exactly a minute. Then I explain that 1 minute of their life has just passed – and it is only if they learned the lesson not to waste time in the future that the minute was an investment. It is a simple and hard-hitting message.

One of the other questions I ask my audiences is: 'As a percentage of your working day, how much time do you honestly admit to wasting or allowing other people to waste for you?' I ask them to write the answer down on a small piece of paper, fold it up so that their colleagues cannot see it, and then pass it down the row to the end where I have helpers collect them all. They are then put in a large box and I take 20 out of the box at random and read out the figures. I'd like you to write your figure down now before reading on and please be brutally honest with yourself.

As a percentage of my working day, I waste/allow others to waste ___% of my time.

The average time that those 20 people whose pieces of paper I pulled out of the box admit to wasting or allowing other people to waste for them is a staggering 34 per cent of their working day. What was your figure?

If you really want to double your sales, then one of the first and simplest things you can do is stop wasting time and, as a result, create more selling time.

Here is another exercise for you. Exercise 2.1 (overleaf) consists of two pages. The first is divided into two columns headed **Ways I waste my time** and **How I will deal with this in future**.

On the second page, the columns are headed **Ways I allow others to waste my time** and **How I will deal with this in future**. Having read the following notes, please complete these pages (Exercise 2.1) either now or as soon as possible.

Ways you waste your time: Not having your current day fully planned the day before so you spend time planning it.

The solution: I will commit to planning every following day before I leave the office.

Ways you waste your time: Reading an irrelevant magazine.

The solution: I will commit to only reading relevant trade magazines in the office and only when I am taking a break.

Ways you waste your time: Shuffling business cards to see who you could telephone and who you would most like to telephone, instead of calling them all.

The solution: Start calling them right away and call them all. If you are never going to call them, dispose of their cards so you never shuffle them again.

How you allow others to waste your time: They come over to your desk with a cup of coffee in their hand and want to chat to you while they are drinking it and you are working.

The solution: Tell them politely that you have goals you want to achieve today and cannot spare the time.

How you allow others to waste your time: They come and ask you for advice and say something like, 'What would you do in this situation?'

The solution: You reply, 'Why don't you go and think this through first, come back to me with your solution and I'll see if I agree.'

How you allow others to waste your time: Somebody invites you out for a spot of lunch and a chat about their holiday.

The solution: I am not saying lunch is for wimps but if you are going to have lunch, either have it with a customer or client, whilst networking, with colleagues to brainstorm some challenges you are facing or alone and reading a useful book at the same time.

exercise 2.1

Ways I waste my time	How I will deal with this in future

If you prefer not to write in this book, this form and all others are available to download at www.bruceking.co.uk/doubleyoursales

exercise 2.1 (cont.)

Ways I allow others to waste my time	How I will deal with this in future

If you prefer not to write in this book, this form and all others are available to download at www.bruceking.co.uk/doubleyoursales

When I carry out this exercise with people in a Master Class, the average time they decide they waste shoots up from the 34 per cent before they had carried out this exercise to an even more staggering 55 per cent! How did you do? How much extra time are you going to have available to you now? How much more are you going to be selling as a result of not wasting your time or allowing others to waste it for you?

2 The fear factor and time management

I have already discussed fear with you, and now I want to relate it just to time management. I spend a lot of time in workshops questioning people as to why they waste time. I hear a lot of excuses but the one major reason why people waste time is rarely admitted until I finally mention it. That reason is *fear*!

Fear freezes people and stops them taking the action they should be taking. The moment you start feeling fear it connects with all the other fearful situations you have stored in your subconscious mind, and the more fear that comes up, the more non-positive you feel about everything that is going on around you. Maybe you can relate to the following story I was told by a workshop attendee when we discussed fear.

Susan told me that she had taken a large order from a new customer and really wanted to make a good impression. To that end, she took the order straight back to the office and ran a check to make sure that she could fulfil all the order requirements in the time frame promised to the customer. At 11.30 in the morning she realised she had made a terrible mistake. Two of the 15 items ordered were out of stock and could not be delivered on time and she had quoted a lower price than she should have on another.

She described herself as being in a state of shock and terrified of calling the customer and admitting the errors. She froze. She knew that the sooner she called was probably best, but she could not face making that call right away. The more she thought about it, the worse the implications became – a little like the story I told you earlier about Farmer Jones. She had non-positive words and imaginary conversations running through her mind. She pictured herself sitting at her office desk in a flood of tears with her boss reprimanding her, and the longer she thought about it, the worse she felt. She did not make the call that day and did very little other work either.

That evening she ate a hurried meal, went to bed early, slept badly and had awful dreams relating to her sales situation. The following morning when she arrived in the office, she finally plucked up the courage to make the call. She apologised and explained that, in her eagerness to serve her customer well and promptly, she had made some statements immediately when she should have checked first with her office. Then she asked the customer what he would like to do next. He simply replied that she had made a really good impression on him, that he could wait the extra two weeks for delivery of the two items which were out of stock, and that the price difference on the other item would be OK. He also thanked her for being so apologetic, said he was concerned she seemed so upset and assured her they would be doing lots of business together in the future.

The moral to the story is simply that things are rarely ever as bad as you think they are going to be, but the more you think about them the worse the situation becomes in your mind. So here is my second most effective time management technique:

Do the things you fear most first.

When you do this and get the fearful things out of the way first, the rest of the day becomes an absolute joy.

- Do you dislike or fear cold calling but have to do it? Do you currently put it off until late in the day and sometimes leave the calls until the following day? All the time you delay, the fact you have to do it is still lurking in your subconscious mind and playing havoc with what should be a positive state.

- Do you have some customers that you do not get on with too well and who tend to give you a hard time when you call them? When will you call them now?
- Do you get complaints from time to time? When will you deal with them now?

Here is what you should do when you carry out your planning for the following day's activities. List everything that you have to do, and then prioritise them in order of their fear factor. Those you fear most go to the top of the list and are carried out in that order. If, during that day, something else arises that has to be dealt with and is fearful, do it right away.

3 The ISWAT technique

You have one overriding primary goal right now, which is to double your sales in a timeframe specified by you. So here is my final time management technique. The ISWAT technique is based on the premise that whatever action you take is either moving you towards your goals or moving you away from them. That is so very simple – and so very true.

You need another pad of about 15 adhesive notes, but choose an alternative colour to yellow for this technique. Then write on them as I have illustrated below.

> **ISWAT I am doing now or about to do going to help me achieve my goals?**

Place these alongside your yellow PDP adhesive notes where you will come across them frequently during the course of the day. Every time you are about to start on a new task or project, *read the ISWAT note*! Ask yourself the question, 'Is what I am doing now or about to do going to help me achieve my goals?'

If the answer is 'yes', you have three choices. You can do it right away, you can allocate some specific time to do it later, or you may be fortunate enough to be able to delegate it to someone else, if that is appropriate.

If the answer is 'No, it is not going to help me achieve my goals', you have only one choice – dump it and dump it right away.

If it is another cup of coffee you are going to make – do not make it! If you are going to go and have a chat with a colleague about something unrelated to your goals – do not! If you are about to make a telephone call unrelated to achieving your goals – do not make the call! Focus only on what is going to help you to double your sales. If it is an incoming telephone call from somebody you know who just wants to have a chat – politely hang up.

If you are looking at an e-mail that contains information you think you might look at later in case it just might be of some use in the future – delete it. If it is a piece of paper with some information on it which you think might be of use some time in the future, do not put it in the pile on your desk with other papers. Put it in the waste bin or shred it! If it is a magazine article you were about to read that is unrelated to your goal but the headline grabbed your attention – that goes in the bin too! Only keep what you instantly know will help you to achieve your goals.

You have possibly heard the expression 'Clutter on the desk is clutter in the mind'. Once your conscious mind has seen an item of information, the fact that it exists is stored in your subconscious mind amongst the huge pile of other 'might do' information that is already stored there. It interferes with your focus. Clearing your desk and filing or hiding all this information in a filing cabinet or drawer does not help either. The subconscious mind still knows of its existence. It has to be destroyed! Of course you may occasionally destroy something that could have been of some use but that is nowhere near as bad as storing everything, just in case you might want to refer to it.

❝ clutter interferes with your focus ❞

How many e-mails and other forms of correspondence do you receive every day? How quickly do people expect a response from you? Are you expected to justify every decision or recommendation you ever make with a mass of data to back them up?

I feel very strongly that we live in an age of information overload, unnecessarily rapid response requests and an irrational need to justify decisions or recommendations because so much information could be available to support these, if we could find the time to research it.

The main cause of information overload is probably the internet. It is so easy to send an e-mail with attachments and at virtually no cost. So we are deluged with information that somebody thinks may be relevant to us; but the sender does not really care if it is or not because the time and cost of sending information is negligible. If we still worked in an age when people had to type and send letters written in correct English, with brochures and other accompanying information, I believe the flow of information we receive would be cut by approximately 90 per cent and we would only receive information absolutely relevant to us. I also believe that we are expected to reply to e-mails and telephone calls far too rapidly. It is as if the person who is expecting the response has no respect for our time whatsoever. What is this doing to us as motivated and successful people with goals to achieve? Well, according to a recent survey conducted by my staff, 80 per cent of salespeople worked weekends, 74 per cent worked whilst on annual leave and 36 per cent had daily contact with their offices either by telephone or e-mail. Fifty-eight per cent never took any exercise. How do you deal with this? Very simply and effectively – by using the ISWAT technique.

I also believe that we have come to expect to justify our decisions with data, even to ourselves. We have lost the art of using our most powerful and effective decision-making tool, which is our 'gut feeling'. Take a leaf out of Richard Branson's books and his philosophy on business. Richard is one of the wealthiest and most successful business people on the planet and he was recently quoted as saying: 'I never call in the accountants before making a decision. I make my decisions based on my gut feelings and then call in the accountants to make it work.' Using the ISWAT technique is going to give you back your belief and trust in your gut feelings too.

The combination of these three techniques, applied diligently day by day, will create so much additional time for you. Combined with the other techniques you will learn week by week, you will easily double your sales!

Why people buy

Now let's take a look at why people buy – and in particular the fact that features and benefits do *not* sell!

My favourite definition of selling which I wrote over 20 years ago is:

Exposing companies and individuals to problems they never maybe knew they had and to opportunities they maybe never knew existed, and then showing them how your product or service can help them solve the problems and exploit the opportunities, and getting them to buy.

It does *not* say: 'Exposing companies and individuals to features and benefits' because features and benefits do not motivate people to action!

If you lead with features and benefits, your prospect is most unlikely to be able to relate those to their situation, either because they are not immediately relevant or, more likely, because your prospect has other things on their minds and you have not yet caught their interest sufficiently.

Yes, of course you must know the features and benefits of your product or service, but you talk about those much later in the sales process when you have exposed the problems and opportunities. We shall discuss this in more detail in a later Master Class. First of all, let's take this concept a stage further and look at the real reasons people buy.

People buy for emotional reasons

People buy for emotional reasons and sometimes, just sometimes, need logical reasons to justify their decision. Think about some of your own buying decisions for a moment. Did you ever go out and buy a new pair of shoes when you had plenty already and your favourite pair just needed new heels? But you bought a new pair anyway because you just love new shoes and they make you feel good? Maybe you justified your decision on the basis that if someone saw your bright, shiny, new shoes with the designer name tag, you would create a better impression.

Did you ever buy a new car when there was nothing at all wrong with your current model, but the feel and smell of a new car really makes you feel wonderful? Perhaps you justified your decision on the basis that a new, more expensive, luxury car would impress your clients and they would be more likely to do business with you.

I am sure you can think of lots of examples of when you bought something for emotional reasons and sometimes justified them with a logical reason. My own little foible is that I always buy new socks to wear whenever I am speaking at a conference, seminar or workshop. I just love wearing new socks and my logical reason for spending hundreds of pounds a year on new socks, is because they make me feel so good that I believe I will speak much better and therefore attract even more speaking work. I am also a little paranoid that if I do not wear new socks, I may not feel so good and may not speak well, which leads me on to the next key point.

The two fundamental emotional buying reasons are **to avoid pain** and **to be happy**. Which of those do you think is the greatest buying motivator? Pain or happiness? The answer is **to avoid pain**.

I will use an analogy to demonstrate this point. Let's suppose that you wake up one morning feeling just a little depressed. You probably do not telephone the doctor, insist on an emergency appointment and demand a prescription for a 'happy pill'. There are many other ways you can cheer yourself up. You can go to a movie, go out for a drink or lunch with some friends, read an amusing book or just get on with the day and put up with a little bit of depression. You know that if you get on with your life the depression will probably soon lift and you will not need to be seeking out a therapist to help you.

Compare that situation to waking up one morning with a very bad pain in your head. You take a couple of painkillers but the pain does not go away and, in fact, it gets worse. An half-hour or so later it is so bad that you telephone the doctor for an emergency appointment. When you see the doctor, you literally beg for a prescription for some drug that is going to take this pain away and seek reassurance that there is not something seriously wrong with you.

At some Master Classes people challenge me and suggest that happiness can indeed be a motivator and that pain is not necessarily the more powerful of the two. On one occasion a delegate produced a list he had taken from another sales book, which showed the main motivational reasons why people buy. The following are a few from that list:

- It is fashionable.
- It looks good.
- It is a status symbol.
- It improves health.
- It makes somebody love them.
- It fulfils an ambition.
- It provides security.

I went down the list with the group one item at a time and asked them these questions:

- Would somebody who was concerned about being fashionable be more likely to buy because something made them feel fashionable or because they were scared of being seen as unfashionable (**PAIN**)?
- Would somebody who liked status symbols be more likely to buy because something was a status symbol, or because people would not feel they had any status if they did not have one (**PAIN**)?
- Would somebody who was concerned about being loved be more likely to buy to make someone love them, or because if they did not buy it, they believed somebody would not love them (**PAIN**)?

- Would somebody who was concerned about security be more likely to buy because they now had steel shutters on their windows which kept people out, or because they were petrified of being burgled or raped (**PAIN**)?

By the time I had finished, there was not one person who did not agree that from that point on they would always focus on the pain because pain is indeed the most powerful motivator. Therefore, wherever possible, we want to identify where a customer or potential customer is experiencing problems which are giving them pain. Once we have identified those painful situations and have shown the customer how we can take the pain away, we are far less likely to meet objections to what we are proposing and should have little or no difficulty in closing the sale. In fact the customer should almost be begging to do business with us.

ff pain is indeed the most powerful motivator jj

Now let us also not forget that opportunities are the next best motivator. If you can also expose your customers to opportunities they never knew existed as well as problems they never knew they had, then you have an even better case. Of course in some cases, the opportunity is simply the solution to their pain or problem, but until you have identified the pain, the opportunity does not have such a significant impact.

Here is what I would like you to do next, and you may wish to do it right away or at a more convenient time. It would be preferable to carry out this exercise with several of your colleagues so that you can brainstorm the answers. I would like you to identify every pain you have ever been able to solve for a customer and every opportunity you have been able to present to a customer, and create a question that might expose those problems and opportunities.

Here are some additional and important facts which illustrate why this exercise is so important. About 85 per cent of potential buyers are not looking for a solution to a problem and do not know other opportunities exist. Either that or they do realise they have a problem or know of opportunities but do not believe there is a solution or a cost-effective solution to either solving the problem or exploiting the opportunity. They have therefore decided not to do anything about it. That is obviously a potentially enormous market.

The remaining 15 per cent who realise they have a problem or an opportunity and are looking for a solution are a much smaller market and, because they are already looking, will probably already be speaking to other companies who might provide the solution. So if you are prospecting for new business in this sector, you have a much smaller market and probably a lot of competition already.

It is therefore very obvious that you should be prospecting for new business in the 'don't know they have a problem or an opportunity or have decided to live with the problem or not exploit the opportunity' sector and, in order to do this effectively, you must have a list of questions you can ask that will enable your prospect to realise they have a problem or an opportunity.

Please complete Exercises 2.2 and 2.3 on the following pages now or as soon possible. If you already have some case studies, these should give you examples of how your company has solved problems and helped your clients exploit opportunities in the past. If you visit your competitors' websites, you may well find they have published case studies that could also give you some useful ideas.

exercise 2.2

Pain/problem solved	Question to expose pain/problem

If you prefer not to write in this book, this form and all others are available to download at www.bruceking.co.uk/doubleyoursales

exercise 2.3

Opportunity exposed	Question to expose opportunity

If you prefer not to write in this book, this form and all others are available to download at www.bruceking.co.uk/doubleyoursales

Key action points

- Stop wasting time – do the exercise detailed under this heading.

- Do the things you fear most first. Create your daily action plan on this basis.

- Implement the ISWAT technique.

- Features and benefits don't sell.

- People buy for emotional reasons.

- Pain is a greater motivator than pleasure.

- Carry out Exercises 2.2 and 2.3.

- Continue with the *GAVA double your sales – fast* process daily.

- Study and work on applying the techniques in this Master Class for at least one week before moving on.

3

Prospecting for new business 1
Cold calling for appointments: the professional way

New customers are the lifeblood of all successful businesses.
Dale Carnegie, motivational author and speaker

Most salespeople I know and meet dislike cold calling more so than any other activity they have to undertake. It is my intention that by the end of this Master Class, you will enjoy the challenge of cold calling and become very much more effective. The techniques I am about to teach you have worked for thousands of other salespeople and they can work for you too.

The rules of engagement

If you are telephoning a prospect, either to sell to them or to make an appointment to sell to them, you are 'cold calling', and cold calling can simply be defined as 'a telephone call being made to someone who was not expecting your call'.

It does not matter if you had written to them beforehand and are following up that e-mail or the brochure you sent them. If it was an e-mail, it may not have been opened or even reached them. If it was a letter, it may have been lost in the post or not passed on to them by somebody opening their mail. Even if they had seen it, the content may not have been of interest. It is still a cold call and the rules of engagement apply.

It does not matter if the person you are calling is a referral from another person. There is no guarantee at all that they will remember your name or your company's name when you make the call, even if the person who referred you had told them to expect a call from you. It is still a cold call and the rules of engagement apply.

It does not even matter if they were eagerly expecting your call. If their PA or other gatekeeper has not been informed by them to put you through, it is still a cold call and the rules of engagement apply.

The preparation

Before we engage with the person we are cold calling there is a lot of preparatory work to do; so let's get started.

First of all, let us discuss rejection again because there is no other area in sales where you are likely to suffer rejection as much as when you are cold calling.

Some sales coaches will tell you that rejection has nothing to do with you and that the customer or potential customer is just rejecting your product or service. That's rubbish! I can think of many reasons why someone would reject *you* when you call them, including:

- You pronounced their name incorrectly.
- It was obvious they were very busy and you should have acknowledged that and said you would call back at another time.
- You were rude to them.
- You were rude to their PA or secretary.
- You interrupted them.
- You didn't listen.
- You ignored their 'objections'.

■ You were unprofessional.

■ You spoke badly.

■ You spoke like it was just another cold call you were making.

■ You sounded as if you were reading from a script.

■ You sounded disinterested in what they had to say and just wanted to get on with what you had to say.

■ You didn't seem to understand their issues or know your product or service and what it could do for them.

And the list goes on!

So what I would like you to do is go to Exercise 3.1 on the following page now, or at the next convenient opportunity, and make a list of all the reasons why people may have rejected *you* in the past. Then make a decision as to how to conduct yourself in the future to avoid this ever happening again.

Reasons prospects have rejected *me* in the past – be honest!

_____

_____

_____

_____

_____

_____

_____

_____

_____

_____

_____

_____

_____

_____

_____

_____

_____

_____

_____

_____

_____

If you prefer not to write in this book, this form and all others are available to download at www.bruceking.co.uk/doubleyoursales

Dealing with rejection

Now let us discuss how to deal with rejection if it was not you who was being rejected but rather your product or service.

Instead of thinking about the outcome of your call as being to make a sale or make an appointment, you need to put this into a totally different perspective. When you make a telephone call, no matter how carefully you have done your research into the prospect, 99 per cent of the time you have absolutely no idea whether or not your prospect has any real need for your product or service at that time. So instead of thinking the outcome of your call should be to make a sale or an appointment, you should look at the purpose of your call as being to establish whether or not your prospect has a need for your product or service, either now or in the future. Then, providing you have presented to them professionally and purposefully, you always come out with a positive outcome and you can move on to making the next call in a positive frame of mind.

And finally, remember this:

Rejection never leaves you any worse off than before you were rejected.

It is also important to realise that how you perceive yourself is how others will perceive you too...

Cold callers – bad and good

One of the conscious and subconscious challenges we face when we cold call is based on the fact that we have all been on the receiving end of many terrible cold calls. When I'm in the office and not too busy, I ask for all cold telephone calls to be put through to me. I like listening to what are, in most cases, appalling but occasionally brilliant pitches.

Here are two examples of appalling ones:

Caller: Is that Mr King?

Me: Yes.

Caller: How are you today Mr King? (I simply hate that question from a total stranger on a cold call – it's so very insincere so I said)...

Me: Absolutely awful thank you.

Caller: Excellent! I'm calling from the XYZ Company – would you be interested in buying CCTV?

Me: No.

And the caller hung up!

And here's another...

Caller: I'm calling to speak to the owner of the business.

Me: We have 27,000 shareholders all of whom own the business. Which one would you like to speak with? (That wasn't true – just me being difficult.)

Caller: Oh – any one of the owners who's available.

Me: None of them work here. They are just owners and shareholders. Do you have the name of the person you need to speak with?

Caller: I just wanted to speak with the owner.

Me: What's it about?

Caller: It's private.

Me: Which company do you represent – who are you calling on behalf of please?

Caller: It's private. I can't tell you.

Me: Well I might be able to put you through to someone who could help if you can tell me what it's about.

Caller.   I can't – it's private for the owner.

Me: Tell you what. I'll promise not to tell your boss you told me what it's about. Then when you do, I may be able to put you through to the right person.

There was silence for a while – then they hung up.

The truth of the matter is that good cold callers are so rare that we think we are all tarred with the same brush. We think we know how people are going to react to a cold call before we have even dialled the number and we expect a similar outcome to those who make such bad calls. And what you expect is what you get – most of the time!

Now think back to a time when you received a really excellent cold call, and your positive response, or you listened to a real professional make one and get a positive response. It was a whole different ball game wasn't it!

Let us also dispel one final myth relating to attitude before we move on. I have heard so many people refer to cold calling as 'just a numbers game'. They treat it in the same way as untargeted junk mail. Make the calls in the same old, same old way and eventually someone will say 'yes'. That is absolutely the wrong attitude!

Of course if you keep records, and I will explain how to do this for your own benefit later in this Master Class, then you count the numbers: *but* the numbers can be massively improved upon as you improve your skills. I have coached thousands of telephone sales and marketing people to use the same skills I am teaching you in this Master Class, and in many cases, results have improved by 500 per cent and more!

So from now on, and with the help of this programme, set yourself up to think and act like a true professional cold caller and expect to get great results.

Your office space and equipment

I appreciate that you do not always have complete control over your working environment and, believe me, I have seen telephone salespeople working in some dreadful places in the past. Fortunately this happens far less often nowadays. But if you have a choice, do make sure it is as conducive to high and successful productivity as possible.

Here are some key points:

- You need fresh air – stale air makes you stale.
- It should be not too hot and not too cold – normal body temperature or a tiny bit colder is best.
- Have some uplifting pictures and slogans on the walls, plus your our own 'goal board' – pictures from your goal book representing your goals.
- It should be as quiet as possible so you are not distracted and the prospect is not distracted by background noise.
- You should also have an uncluttered desk; just have all you need close by for the task in hand.

There are also three other important items.

1 A headset

This is an absolute essential for cold calling or indeed when spending any time on the telephone. You must have your hands free to be able to carry out other tasks whilst you are making your calls without holding the telephone between your shoulder and cheek. Not only will this give you a stiff neck but, more importantly, it affects your posture, your voice and the way you communicate and come across to your prospect. It affects how they visualise you.

When you are speaking on the telephone, my number 1 rule is that you should always act as if you were actually sitting down with that prospect. You never do anything you would not do if you were not there and you do everything you would do if you were there. You wear the same expression on your face as if you were there and you gesticulate and use mannerisms as if you were there. You cannot do that with a telephone in one hand and a mouse or pen in the other – or indeed juggling the two. I have acted as a consultant to many organisations who have achieved a 20 per cent plus increase in sales just by replacing handsets with headsets.

2 A mirror

You should have a mirror so that you can check the expression on your face. And put a notice above it with the word **SMILE** written in bold print. And smile!

3 A monitoring system – actually two!

The first of your two systems is a customer relationship management (CRM) system. This is used to keep track of your prospects, their contact details, details of their business, the key people around them such as their secretary or PA, your progress to date with them, date and time of next call and any other important points you should make note of, all accessible in one place.

There are very effective CRM computer-based systems you can use or it could be as simple as a card box system. Of course the computer-based systems are going to be far more sophisticated than a box stuffed with index cards, but I know some really top salespeople who still use a card box system and are amongst the top performers in their field. As Zig Ziglar, the American self-help author once said, *'I don't care what system you use, just so long as you have a system!'*

The second system is a results monitor (RM for short). These are built into some of the most sophisticated CRM systems but, in most cases, are not as comprehensive and effective as a paper-based system or a spreadsheet. It will not take you long to set one up and the benefits can be extraordinary.

The purpose of a results monitor is to track your results at each stage of the telephone call; to show you areas where you may need to coach yourself or get coached on the particular skill needed for that part of the process; to monitor how you are improving and, most importantly, to know the results you are getting. In a moment I will go through the structure of the paper-based system or spreadsheet, but first of all, and to demonstrate why it is so important, let's go right to the end.

Let's suppose that you have been tracking the results of your cold calling for 20 hours. From the RM system, you have worked out the following statistics:

- It took two dials to get an answer from anyone to the calls you make.
- It took four dials to get through to a decision maker's PA or secretary.
- It took three conversations with a PA or secretary to get put through to a decision maker.
- It took five conversations with a decision maker to get an appointment to see one of them.

Your statistics from your meeting records show that the average meeting, whether you sell at all of them or not, generates a sale to the value of £2400, or sales over the lifetime value of that customer of £2400.

So working that backwards, it takes 60 cold telephone calls to earn £2400 which equates to £40 per cold call.

Of course your statistics will be different for a number of reasons, your sales process may be rather different and you will be working out your own statistics in the future. But let us suppose this data was yours. Does it shed a rather different light on the picture when you work out that you have earned £40 per cold call? And to put it in a totally different perspective...

Suppose I were to pay you £40 every time you picked up the telephone and dialled a number. What time would you get into the office in the morning and start cold calling? How often would you take a break? How often would you wander off for a conversation with a colleague? How long would you take for lunch and how late would you stay into the evening? And ... has the penny dropped?

On the following page you will find an example of an RM spreadsheet. It might work for you as it is, or you may need to redesign it for your particular purpose. For example you might want to add columns for:

VML = Voice Mail Message Left
VMR = Voicemail Messages Returned
DMNA = Decision Maker Not Available
PCB = Permission To Call Back

Sample RM chart

DIAL	CONTACT	DM	INTRO	PITCH	APPT. MADE	SALE	SALE VALUE (£)
TOTALS							

Time started: Time finished:

This template is available to download at www.bruceking.co.uk/doubleyoursales

It is up to you to adjust this sample to make it work for you.

What other columns would you add that best suit your situation and will help you to monitor your results? Write them down and then prepare your own RM sheets. You could use an Excel spreadsheet or any other program that is appropriate for the purpose.

Now let us take a look at how you can interpret the results from an RM. Here is an example:

Appointment setting RM

DIAL	CONTACT	DM	INTRO	PITCH	APPT MADE
60	45	12	6	3	1

We could deduce the following from these results:

- If this is a business-to-business scenario, then this is not a good list if 15 were 'gone away'.

- You need to improve your skills with PAs and secretaries to get them to put you through. Of course the DM (decision maker) could be out or in a meeting and you might wish to add a column to the RM sheet headed DMNA (Decision Maker Not Available) and another for PCB (Permission to Call Back).

- You should examine your opening statement. Fifty per cent of decision makers were not allowing you to continue.

- Ask yourself is one appointment in three pitches acceptable? Could it be improved upon?

Here is another example. What will you deduce from these results? (Answers not supplied.)

■■■■■■■■ Telephone selling RM

DIAL	CONTACT	DM	INTRO	PITCH	SALE	SALE VALUE £
60	59	12	11	3	0	0

Researching the prospect

This Master Class is not about marketing, so I am going to assume that you have already identified your prospects and have a substantial list of these to call, which you will be adding to on a regular basis.

It is very obvious the more you know about your prospects, the more likely you are to get a positive result when you telephone them. The amount of research you do is dependent on various factors which include the value of the sale, the long-term value of the customer and also how appropriate the research will be with regard to other prospects operating in the same or similar sectors.

And just to remind you again – people buy for emotional reasons, the most important being to avoid or rid themselves of pain, so ideally, you are looking for the following information.

■ General problems that companies in the *general* sector you are selling to will be experiencing and that you have been able to solve for similar companies in the past.

■ General problems that companies in the *specific* sector you are selling to will be experiencing and that you have been able to solve for similar companies in the past.

- Specific problems that companies in the *general* sector you are selling to will be experiencing and that you have been able to solve for similar companies in the past.

- Specific problems that companies in the *specific* sector you are selling to will be experiencing and that you have been able to solve for similar companies in the past.

You are also looking for information as to how you have been able to show your prospect opportunities to exploit that they may not have been aware of.

I am sure I do not have to tell you that the best and easiest form of research that is available to you if you are operating in the business-to-business (B2B) market, and even to some extent in the business-to-consumer (B2C) market, is the internet. When I first started in sales I would have given my right arm to be able to get hold of the information that companies now publish on their websites. What is now available at the click of a mouse would have saved me countless hours of research, frustration and telephone calls.

❝ the best form of research available to you is the internet ❞

Your competitors will also often have case studies on their websites showing problems they have been able to solve that maybe had not occurred to you. They will also have them in their brochures and other promotional literature and I'm sure that you could find ways of obtaining copies of these.

Here is something else that I must mention. Do you employ someone to set appointments for you? If you do, then please do not fall into the trap of thinking they do not need to know very much and their job is just to make an appointment. If you want them making regular appointments for you, they need to know at least half as much as you do by the time you have finished this series of Master Classes. If they come across as knowledgeable and do not know the answers to everything they are asked, that is the perfect opportunity for them to say something like:

That's a question that's a little out of my depth Mrs Jones. Our sales consultant is the best person to answer that question for you and would have other important information relative to your situation to show and explain to you. So when could we book in an appointment for her to see you please? I know Jane has a free slot on Tuesday at 11 am and Thursday at 3 pm. Which of those is good for you?

So maybe you should be coaching your appointment setter a lot more if you use one. Maybe even invest in a copy of this book for them to study.

Preparing your approach

Now let's look at preparing your approach and let us discuss 'scripts' first of all, because I know that 'script' is a word and a concept that a lot of people react badly to when I tell them to write one.

Imagine the scene. The Globe Theatre is packed with an audience eagerly anticipating a performance of William Shakespeare's *The Merchant of Venice*. Meanwhile, behind the curtains, a group of actors are in quiet discussion.

'Anyone ever done *The Merchant of Venice* before?' asks one.
'No but I've got a vague idea of how it goes', says another.
'Can't be that difficult. I'm sure we'll wing our way through it
  OK', says yet another.
'Let's face it, the audience won't know if we got it wrong
  anyway', says the last.

And so they go on stage, not ever having studied the script, totally unprepared – and it's a complete and utter mess!

Of course that would not happen. So why would any salesperson not know precisely what they are going to say during a telephone call or a sales presentation? Why would they not know what questions they were going to ask? Why would they not know all the questions they were likely to be asked and have answers prepared? Why, why, why would they not have a script to work to and rehearse, rehearse, rehearse? Let's face it – when we're selling,

❝ when we're selling, we're on stage ❞

we're on stage! And the larger the value of the sale and/or the long-term value of the customer or client – the more rehearsals are needed.

But let us also be clear: the purpose of writing a script is *not* to follow it word for word and refuse to be sidetracked. The purpose is:

■ To know precisely what you are going to say in your opening statement to arouse interest and to get the prospect to want to continue with a *conversation,* and

■ To have questions prepared to identify pain and opportunities whilst having a *conversation,* and

■ To have answers prepared to all the questions that you know, from your experience and the experience of others, are likely to be asked during that *conversation,* and

■ To know how to respond effectively so the prospect wants to continue with the *conversation* and ultimately agree to your proposal.

The only difference between a salesperson on the telephone and an actor on stage is that the actor cannot walk on stage with their script. They have to learn it off by heart. When you are selling a product, service or appointment on the telephone, you have the advantage that you can keep your script or the key points from your script nearby to refer to. Not so in face-to-face sales presentations!

Only when you have written the near perfect script and know each section of it off by heart can you relax and have a *conversation* knowing you can handle just about everything that comes up during that conversation. So let us look at how best to structure your opening statement and you can tailor these approaches and the follow up, whether you are calling to make an appointment or to sell.

You will have noticed I have used the word 'conversation' frequently in the preceding paragraphs. Let me expand upon this...

I mentioned earlier in this Master Class that we have all been on the receiving end of numerous dreadful cold calls and the last thing you want is to appear to be from the same mould. The impression you want to give as fast as you possibly can is that you are pleasant, knowledgeable and could be a trusted adviser and an asset to your prospect's business – even if you are simply selling toilet paper. And that was meant with the greatest of respect to janitorial suppliers. My own janitorial supplier's representative knows more about Health & Safety issues than most others I have met. He is my trusted adviser!

In order to come across in the best possible way you must have a professional, enthusiastic but relaxed approach; engage the prospect's interest as quickly as possible by appearing knowledgeable and an authority on your subject; and engage them in a conversation as quickly as possible that will enhance your reputation with them and put you head and shoulders above your competition.

Having said that, I should also emphasise that you are not setting yourself up or should not be allowing yourself to be set up to be intimidated, pushed around or used as an unpaid consultant by the prospect. Indeed the opposite applies. As an expert in your field, you deserve and should expect respect.

So a word of caution here, and meant with the greatest of respect to you. If you are not an expert in your field, then you owe it to yourself and your prospects to become an expert as fast as you possibly can! Do what is necessary to justify that qualification – fast!

First things first – you must have a goal for a call

It is absolutely essential to have a clear intention as to what you want the ideal result of the call to be. Without that, you cannot possibly frame the correct questions that will get you that result. You should also have several satisfactory fallback positions so you get something out of the call that will leave you in a positive frame of mind. The result you want could be one or more of the following:

- It could be to establish there is or is not a need for your product or service, now or in the future.
- It could be to establish who is the person you need to be speaking with if it is not the person you call.
- It could be to establish when the appropriate person will be available.
- It could be to make a sale or make an appointment.
- It could be to get an agreement to talk them through an online presentation.
- It could be to get an agreement they will visit your website and when to call back.
- It could be to get an agreement that literature or other information can be sent and when you can call back for a review.

Do you have anything to add to that list? The key point here is to know what you want to achieve from the call and have satisfactory fallback positions if you do not achieve the number one goal. That way, you always come out with a positive result. So now, or when it is convenient, complete Exercise 3.2 on possible positive outcomes you could expect from a call.

exercise 3.2

What are all the possible positive outcomes you could
expect from a call to a prospect?

_____

_____

_____

_____

_____

_____

_____

_____

_____

_____

_____

_____

_____

_____

_____

_____

_____

_____

_____

_____

If you prefer not to write in this book, this form and all others are
available to download at www.bruceking.co.uk/doubleyoursales

The silent close

Before we move on, there is another important concept I need to introduce to you right now – and I do mean *important*. It is the *'silent close'*. The rule is, whenever you ask a closing question, you keep quiet. The first person to speak inevitably loses.

Now you might think that this belongs in a later Master Class entitled *Closing the sale*; so let me explain why it is relevant from this point on, and why I will be mentioning it throughout the following Master Classes.

By 'closing question' I mean any question you ask, at any stage of the sales process, that will move you on in the sales process. Whenever you ask that question that moves you on – that 'closing question' – you keep quiet, for two reasons. Firstly, because the other person may be thinking of their response and it is rude to interrupt someone when they are thinking. Secondly, because the first person to speak after the closing question has been asked is at a disadvantage! So let me repeat that instruction. Whenever you ask a closing question – keep quiet!

❝ whenever you ask a closing question – keep quiet ❞

Here is a great story about when I recently used the silent close. I was in the process of selling an in-house sales training programme to a large organisation. I had two previous meetings with the Sales Director who seemed keen to go ahead, and now I had what I planned to be the final meeting with the Managing Director. My aim was to close the deal at that meeting and I am sure you realise that when you are selling sales training, you have to demonstrate you know what you are doing.

I used my normal process which was to establish rapport, summarise the problems they had outlined to me, summarised my solutions to their problems, and then asked if they were certain my proposals would solve their problems. They agreed they would. And then I asked one of my two favourite closing questions – 'So what happens next?' – followed by the silent close. There was a pause of about 10 seconds and then a neon sign lit up on the MD's forehead. It said: 'He's using the silent close on me!' And a neon sign lit up on my forehead which said: 'I know you know.' And we sat there smiling at each other. From time to time I deliberately looked at my watch, looked up again, made eye contact and smiled. And he smiled back. After 11 minutes and 15 seconds the MD burst out laughing and said: 'Bruce, I just wanted to see how long you could keep that up for.' I said, 'So will we be starting in April or May?' (alternative question close) – followed again by the silent close. Within 5 seconds he said 'April Bruce.' That is the power of the silent close!

So from now on, whenever you ask a closing question, anything that moves you on in the sales process – remember the silent close.

The rules of engagement

Let's start by looking at your opening statements and questions and first of all – How *not* to start a conversation. These are things you should *never* say:

- *'How are you today?'* – It's just so insincere. The only stranger who can convincingly ask me that question is a doctor!
- *'I'm sorry to bother you but...'* Why would you want to have your prospect thinking about being 'bothered'?
- *'I'm sorry to trouble you but...'* Why would you want to have your prospect thinking about being 'troubled'?
- 'Do you have a minute to talk right now?' Why give them the opportunity to say 'no'?
- *'Am I interrupting?'* Why would you want to have your prospect thinking about being 'interrupted'?
- *'Have you heard of us?'* Again – why give the prospect the opportunity to say 'no'? We don't ever want to get a 'no' right at the beginning of a conversation and have our prospect in a non-positive frame of mind.

Those statements and questions may have made you aware of some other 'no-no' opening statements you use as well. If it has, do not use those either.

Effective opening statements and questions

Instead, let's take some examples of effective opening statements and questions. These are varied in style and approach and later in this Master Class we will extend some of these into the actual conversations that followed.

This following example is to someone who might be experiencing a particular problem: 'Good morning John, it's Bruce King calling from the XYZ Company. I'm working with a few other companies in your sector, most of whom seem to be experiencing the same challenges in particular areas of their business. So the reason I'm calling you is to ask if you're open to having a brief chat to see if you're experiencing similar problems. Would that be OK?'

In this next example, the person is a referral who might be experiencing a particular problem: 'Good morning John, it's Bruce King calling. I believe Robert Smith of The Board Company Limited told you to expect my call. Robert mentioned that a particular situation which concerned another Sales Director of a large organisation in a similar business sector to your own, might be of interest to you. Do you have just a few moments to speak right now or would you prefer I called you back at another time?'

This next one is opportunity rather than pain focused: 'Good morning John, it's Jason Smith calling from the XYZ Company. I'm working with a few other companies in your sector, and I've been able to provide them with a simple system that has increased the amount of sales calls their reps are making by up to 37 per cent, with a corresponding increase in sales. So the reason I'm calling you is to ask if you're open to having a brief chat right now to see if that's something you'd be interested in exploring in some more detail. Would that be OK?'

Here is a short one that starts with a question almost immediately: 'Good morning Robert. My name is Mary Wilson from Abbey Office Furniture. I understand you are the person who deals with purchasing office furniture. Is that correct?'

And here's the 'I'm a salesperson' approach – direct and to the point with a clever twist: 'Good morning Peter. I'm Bruce King from Bruce King & Associates and this is a sales call; probably the last thing you want right now, so can I just take one minute of your time to tell you what I do and then you can decide if you want to take another two or three minutes on the phone or hang up. Is that fair?' (Yes) 'Thank you. I help companies whose sales teams are struggling to meet their sales targets, to meet or exceed them in a very short space of time. My question is: what are some of the things you'd want to know before being comfortable enough to invite me in for a face-to-face meeting?' Shortly after they start to speak, you interrupt and say: 'Excuse me interrupting Peter but I have a challenge here. I did say one minute and that's up. Are you sure you want to continue?'

Finally a brief, polite and questioning approach: 'Good morning John, this is Bruce King from the XYZ company. I'm working with a number of other accountants in your area and I'm calling to ask if you're open to discussing a more cost effective and efficient way of handling the storage of clients' files. I was hoping we could ask each other a few questions to see if it's worth spending some more time discussing this at a later date? Would that be OK please?'

Now, or as soon as you are able to, write some of your opening statements and questions (see Exercise 3.3 – overleaf), based on the problems and opportunities you have already identified. When you are happy with them, learn them off by heart.

exercise 3.3

My opening statements and questions

If you prefer not to write in this book, this form and all others are
available to download at www.bruceking.co.uk/doubleyoursales

The conversation

Now let's move on to the presentation or rather the conversation. By now, you are almost certainly seeing how several different approaches can achieve the same desired result – a conversation. Let us take two of these examples and go through the entire presentation. Bear in mind that the salesperson has gone through all the necessary preparatory work and from this point on, is no longer working from a script word for word. They have learned it off by heart and are now using all their knowledge and skills to have a conversation.

In this first example, the prospect is a referral and has a problem. All the salesperson has to do is act very professionally and aim to get the appointment as quickly as possible with the least amount of pressure on the prospect. Here is the conversation:

'Good morning John, it's Bruce King calling. I believe Robert Smith of The Board Company Limited told you to expect my call. Robert mentioned that a particular situation, which concerned another Sales Director of a large organisation in a similar business sector to your own, might be of interest to you. Do you have a few moments right now or would you prefer I called you back at another specific time?'

'No – Robert did mention you when he called me last night, so carry on.'

'Thank you. The issue this organisation had and that Robert thought might interest you was that their salespeople were spending too much time taking orders from existing customers and were not opening enough new accounts. Customers were required to place all orders, including repeat business, through the salesperson, leaving them insufficient time for developing new business. Is that a situation you might also be experiencing John?'

'I am having some concerns in that area. What precisely did you have in mind?'

'Thank you for confirming that John. What happened in that case was we made a detailed study of their current methodology and came up with three ways to maximise the time a salesperson had to spend generating new business, through more effective prospecting and referral systems and ways to motivate them to achieve their targets for new business. We helped them develop some relatively simple internal systems for achieving this and developed a training system for the sales team. The result was that over the following six months, the customer base increased by 23 per cent and sales increased by 38 per cent. Would that kind of result impress you John?'

'It couldn't fail to could it? Of course budgets are tight right now so a lot would depend upon the cost and whether or not you could achieve the same result for us.'

'At this stage, I really couldn't say. We have achieved the same results – and better – with similar organisations to yours but I'd need to know a lot more about your business before I could be certain. What I'd like to do, if it's OK with you, is meet with you in person, discuss your situation in a lot more detail and then we'd both be a lot clearer as to what could or could not be achieved. When could we arrange that – what slots do you have in your diary next week John?'

In this next example, the salesperson has three 'pains' ready to mention which are specific to the business sector the prospect operates in. This is not a referral – it's a cold call. It goes like this:

'Good morning John, it's Bruce King calling. Thanks for taking my call. I'm working with a number of other companies operating in your business sector who have all been experiencing significant problems in three areas of their business. Do you have a few moments right now for me to tell you what they are and for us to ask each other a few questions to see if it's worth continuing with this conversation?.

'I've got a couple of minutes max.'

'Thank you. There are three main areas they are having difficulty with:

1   The sales team are not meeting targets for generating new customers.

2 The sales team are spending too much time taking small orders from existing customers which are not contributing sufficiently to their overall sales targets, and

3 Because of this, the sales managers and the sales team are frustrated and demotivated.

Can you relate to any of these issues John?'

'I certainly have some concerns in two of those areas. What precisely do you have in mind?'

'Can you tell me more specifically about those two situations and how they are affecting your business? Naturally it's totally confidential.'

A conversation develops culminating in a request from the prospect:

'So what can you do for us?'

'I've no idea right now John. What happened in one of the situations I was involved in is that we made a detailed study of their current methodology and came up with three ways to maximise the time a salesperson had to spend generating new business, through more effective prospecting and referral systems *and* ways to motivate them to achieve their targets for new business. We helped them develop some relatively simple internal systems for achieving this and developed a training system for the sales team. The result was that over the following six months, the customer base increased by 23 per cent and sales increased by 38 per cent. Would that kind of result impress you John?'

'It couldn't fail to could it? Of course budgets are tight right now so a lot would depend upon the cost and whether or not you could achieve the same result for us.'

'At this stage, I really couldn't say. We have achieved the same results – and better – with similar organisations to yours but I'd need to know a lot more about your business before I could be certain. What I would like to do, if it's OK with you, is meet with you in person, discuss your situation in a lot more detail and then we'd both be a lot clearer as to what could be achieved.

When could we arrange that – what slots do you have in your diary next week John?'

In this next example, the prospect is also a cold call and was initially very resistant. The salesperson could easily have given in at any stage of this call, but used questioning skills and objection handling skills to create the opportunity to close on an appointment in a subsequent call. Here's how the call went...

'John Smith speaking.'

'Good morning John. My name is Mary Jones from Abbey Office Furniture. I understand you are the person who deals with purchasing office furniture. Is that correct?'

'Yes but we don't need anything right now.'

'I understand and I appreciate your honesty John. I'm calling because Abbey Office Furniture would like to be the company you look to when you do have a need for furniture. Our customers love our mix of quality, design and competitive pricing. Could you please tell me how we could position ourselves to earn the opportunity to be considered?'

'Top of the list would be pricing. You'd have to be able to offer the most competitive prices. Why don't you just put a catalogue and price list in the post?'

'John, let's assume we could offer you the lowest or, at very least, most competitive pricing. What other factors would be strongly considered before you decided who you would place a future order with?'

'Can you just send me some information in the mail?'

'I'd be very happy to do that John. I have a tremendous amount of different literature here, some of which may not be of any interest to you at all. Do you mind if I ask you a few questions so I can just send what I believe will be relevant?'

'Go on then.'

'Thank you. When do you anticipate you might need to invest in more furniture and is there a particular project you have in mind?'

'We'll be fitting out a new telesales department for 20 operators in about nine months' time.'

(At this point the salesperson asked a series of questions relating to the type of layout they were anticipating and the type of furniture required. Then:)

'John, I'm going to put some brochures together today. May I make an appointment to bring them round and go through the information with you? Can we organise that?'

'No. Just put them in the post.'

'OK. I'll do that. How long do you need to review what I send you?'

'Forty-eight hours I suppose.'

'OK, so I'll call you on Monday John, and here is what I would like to happen. If you are comfortable with this approach, I'd like you to say that you have read through the brochures and particularly my notes on our free design service and there's absolutely no reason for us to meet. *Or* you can tell me that there is some interest, in which case I'd like you to call me in for a face-to-face meeting. Is that fair John?'

'Very fair indeed.'

'Thank you. You have a lovely weekend and we'll speak on Monday.'

'Thank you Mary!'

On Exercise 3.4 (overleaf), write the key points that you simply must bring up in your conversation and some questions that will enable you to do so.

exercise 3.4

Key points	Questions to ask

If you prefer not to write in this book, this form and all others are available to download at www.bruceking.co.uk/doubleyoursales

How to work through 'gatekeepers'

Now let us talk about gatekeepers because you are not always going to get put through immediately to the person you want to speak to. Many of your prospects will have someone in place to protect them from cold calls and so a great deal of your success is going to depend upon how you deal with the gatekeepers.

The first thing to understand is that the gatekeeper is not a nasty, snarling, ill-tempered, difficult person, hired only for their ability to destroy the confidence and livelihoods of salespeople who cold call. They are usually very pleasant, competent people with a variety of other responsibilities, and they would not have their jobs if they were not pleasant and competent. It is just that one of their roles is to prevent their boss from being constantly inter-rupted by cold calls from people they have no interest in talking to. Their job is to screen calls and only put through those that they are convinced could be of interest. So do not start off on the wrong foot and expect them to be horrible to you because what you think is what you get – most of the time!

❝ the gatekeeper's job is to screen calls ❞

The first rule of dealing with gatekeepers is to be pleasant, pro-fessional and friendly. You want to make them your friend, or at least not alienate them from the moment you start to speak. That does not however mean grovelling or being over friendly and gushing!

Here are some examples of effective ways to negotiate with the gatekeeper, starting with a very simple approach, as if you are calling to speak to your best friend, through to an eventual, veiled threat when all else has failed.

'Is John in?'

'Who's that?'

'Bruce King – can you put me through to John please.'

And they put you through.

Or

'John Smith, please'.

'Who's speaking?'

'Bruce King – can you put me through to John please.'

'Does he know you?'

'Yes he does.' (He doesn't – but never mind.)

And they put you through.

Or

'John Smith, please'

'Who's speaking?'

'Bruce King – who am I speaking with please?'

'I'm June – John's PA.'

'Hello June – can you put me through to John please.'

'Does he know you?'

'Yes he does.'

'What company are you from?'

'Bruce King & Associates.'

'And what's it in connection with?'

Now there are several approaches you can take from here. For example:

'Robert from the XYZ company recommended I call and he is expecting me.'

Or

'I'm working with a few other companies in your sector, and I've been able to provide them with a simple system that has increased the amount of sales calls their reps are making by up to 77 per cent, with a corresponding increase in sales. It's something I'm sure John would want to know about, so can you put me through please June.'

Or

'He wanted me to call him a few days after I sent him some suggestions/proposals/confidential information and he would have received that three days ago. So can you put me through please June.'

Or

'I have some information for him about some of the problems his competitors are having and which I'm sure he'd like to know about. So can you put me through please June.'

Another completely different approach you can build in if you are having difficulty getting through – and you can introduce this at any time in any of these conversations – is to throw the gatekeeper off balance. They basically have four questions they are trained to ask you. These are:

'What's your name?'

'What company are you calling from?'

'Does he know you?'

'What's it in connection with?'

Asking them questions that don't fit into that framework can really throw them. So ask questions or respond to questions like this:

If they say – 'What's it about?' , you say

'I'd be happy to tell you June but it's important I speak with him directly.'

Or

'I'm not really sure, which is why I need to speak to John.'

If they say – 'What are you selling?', you could say

'I don't understand.'

Or

'Does John want to sell something to me?'

Or

'What's the weather like there June?'

Or

'Is this going to take long June, because I'm calling long distance?'

Or

'What else do you need to know about me personally before you put me through June?'

Or

'June, if you were me, and you had some really important information for John and a couple of questions for him, what would you do now?'

And as a last resort when you know there's no way they are going to put you through – ever – no matter how many times you call back, you can take the risk of sounding rather more confrontational. So you could say:

'June, what are you hoping to achieve by not putting me through to John?'

Or

'June, are you willing to put your company at risk of losing a lot of money by not putting my call through?'

Or

'OK, in that case June – may I please take your full name so that when somebody from your organisation complains to my boss they didn't get to speak with me, I can give them the full name of the contact I did speak to?'

These last examples are not the ideal way to work with a gatekeeper, but if all else has failed and you are not going to be put through, what do you have to lose at this stage?

How to handle voicemail

How many times have you either fought your way past the gate-keeper, or been so happy to have been put through right away, only to be on the receiving end of a voicemail message? Quite often, no doubt. And how many times did you either just hang up or leave a garbled message because you simply were not prepared? Here are three ways to deal with voicemail:

■ Have three 'pains' specific to the prospect's sector ready. These would be the same three you were going to discuss at some point in your conversation anyway. Your message is therefore: *There are three reasons why you should return my call (give the three reasons)* – and leave your name, company name and contact number.

■ You can say: *Deleting this message won't get rid of the three main problems most businesses in your sector are suffering. So please call me back* – and leave your name, company name and contact number.

■ *My name is Bruce King from Bruce King & Associates. My number is 01923 859988. There are three main problems most businesses in your sector are suffering right now. They are one, salespeople are not generating sufficient new business from existing clients, two they're not getting enough new clients and, as a result...* – AND THEN you hang up as if the call was cut off.

As final exercises in this Master Class, now, or as soon as is convenient, turn to the next pages and write down the various ways you are going to work through gatekeepers (Exercise 3.5) and messages you plan to leave on voicemail in the future (Exercise 3.6).

exercise 3.5

How I will work through gatekeepers from now on:

_____

_____

_____

_____

_____

_____

_____

_____

_____

_____

_____

_____

_____

_____

_____

_____

_____

_____

_____

_____

_____

_____

If you prefer not to write in this book, this form and all others are
available to download at www.bruceking.co.uk/doubleyoursales

exercise 3.6

Voice mail messages I will leave from now on:

_____

_____

_____

_____

_____

_____

_____

_____

_____

_____

_____

_____

_____

_____

_____

_____

_____

_____

_____

_____

If you prefer not to write in this book, this form and all others are available to download at www.bruceking.co.uk/doubleyoursales

Pre-approach letters

I am often asked by Master Class delegates whether or not they should send pre-approach letters prior to telephoning a prospect. I do not have strong views on this either way. I do however believe that the better and more professional you become at cold calling, the less the need for a pre-approach letter.

The first thing to consider is the value of the business you are likely to get from a sale to your prospect. If it is a relatively low value, one-off sale, then a pre-approach letter should not be necessary and is probably a complete waste of time and money. If it is a high value sale and/or can lead to long-term business with your prospect, then you may want to consider sending a pre-approach letter. If you do choose to use this approach, then it needs to be an exceedingly good letter and you need to do whatever you can to ensure that it is opened by or passed on to the intended recipient if someone else opens their mail.

My 'killer sales letter' formula

Using this formula myself, I have scored over 25 per cent conversion to appointment at Director level and nearly 50 per cent at senior management level.

Start with a strong heading

This is the first thing that your prospect will read.

Do not write lengthy letters

Lengthy letters with a great deal of text and many paragraphs, no matter how lovingly crafted, will be read by less than 20 per cent of recipients.

Have a maximum of four powerful key points

Select four of your most powerful key points or hooks that should be most relevant and are business sector targeted to your prospect. They should not be the key points that you send to everyone you are writing to across a range of business sectors.

Four key points is the maximum because you are likely to be judged by the recipient on your weakest point.

Place the strongest point at the top of your numbered list

Use numbers rather than bullet points because numbers are easier to refer to in a subsequent telephone conversation. Put your second strongest point or hook last.

Finish with a strong PS

This is the second thing your prospect will read.

Personalise

Hand write the envelope using a fountain pen.

Do not include a brochure

Costs aside, unless you have something stunning and unique to offer which your prospect will almost certainly want to buy, do not send a brochure. Prospects will often make a decision as to whether or not they may want to do business with you based solely on your brochure and if you cannot sell your product or service by mail, focus on selling the appointment.

An example

Here is an example of my 'killer sales letter':

Mr John Smith
XYZ Stationery & Office Equipment PLC
Address

Dear Mr Smith (hand write this salutation with a fountain pen)

Are the four challenges other stationery and office equipment suppliers facing also affecting you?...

I am writing to you because many of our clients in the stationery and office supplies sector have been experiencing the following major challenges for which we have been able to provide solutions.

1 The sales team are not meeting targets for generating new customers.

2 The sales team are spending too much time taking small orders from existing customers which are not contributing sufficiently to their overall sales targets.

3 Significant levels of business are being lost to online stationery and office equipment suppliers.

4 Because of the above three points, the sales managers and the sales team are frustrated and demotivated and profits are falling.

If any of the above issues are relevant to your business and you consider that justifies an informal, 15-minute conversation, please ask your personal assistant to put me through to you when I telephone next Wednesday morning. I have diarised that call for 11 am.

Yours sincerely
Your signature in ink.

P.S. Other companies in the office stationery and equipment sector we have consulted to have increased their customer base by 23 per cent and overall sales by 38 per cent in as little as six months by acting upon our suggestions.

If you are writing a letter like this to a large organisation with a board of directors and layers of management, then you are probably aware of the inertia that exists within larger organisations and the difficulty of gaining their attention and getting to speak with a decision maker. Here is how to overcome this and get the levels of response I mentioned previously.

You send this letter to at least three people within the organisation. For example, if you know that the decision maker and person you should be dealing with is the Sales Director, you send it to them *plus* two other people in more senior positions; possibly the Managing Director and the Finance Director. You include the deadly effective, hand-written, 'with compliments' slip.

This is what you hand write on the 'with compliments' slip:

> *Dear ....*
>
> *Because I am unsure who may be responsible for dealing with this matter, I have taken the liberty of sending a similar letter to Erika Jones and Darren Brown.*
>
> *Your signature.*

Because the same letter has been sent to who you believe are the decision maker's superiors, this letter will be passed on to and be read by the decision maker. They are also far more likely to take a call from you and make an appointment to see you because they will expect to be asked by their superiors for more information on what you had to offer. So your first call is to whom you believe is the decision maker and providing you do speak to them, you can ask them to tell their superiors you have spoken and therefore you will not be calling them yourself.

If they do not take your call, you telephone the next most senior person you wrote to and so on. Eventually, in a significant proportion of cases, someone will take your call and either discuss your letter with you or pass you back down the line again. Rest assured, this technique is indeed deadly effective!

Do you reconfirm or not reconfirm the appointment?

Another question I am often asked by Master Class delegates is whether or not they should reconfirm the appointment the day before or on the morning of the appointment if there is time to do so.

If you have already confirmed the appointment when you first made it, either in writing by snail mail or e-mail, then my answer is an emphatic 'NO'. There is only one good reason you could have for reconfirming and that is to avoid making a journey to visit your prospect, only to find they are either not there or not available. That would indeed save you some time. However, the danger of reconfirming is that you give your prospect the opportunity to cancel.

> **"calling to reconfirm gives your prospect the opportunity to cancel"**

I am the first to admit that in my early days as a salesperson, I used to reconfirm the meeting the day before. When I did that, I very often had the prospect say something like, 'I'm so pleased you called. I was just about to call you and tell you something really important came up and I can't make it. Can you call me next week to reappoint.' When next week came I was very often unable to get through to them and if I did, I had to resell the appointment all over again.

I keep meticulous notes of just about everything that is related to selling activities and early on in my selling career I started to track the results of what happened when I did reconfirm appointments and what happened when I did not. These are the results:

- Out of 620 sales appointments I made during the course of one year and confirmed at the time of making them, I reconfirmed 310 and just turned up for the other 310.

- Of the 310 I reconfirmed, 65 told me they were unable to keep the appointment. Of those 65, I was only able to reappoint 15. So I had 260 meetings.

- Of the 310 I did not reconfirm, nine were unavailable when I arrived. I reappointed all but one. So I had 309 meetings. My closing ratios were almost identical from both groups.

If you would prefer to keep your own records for a while, then please do so. Or you can take my experience as your guideline and do as I do and never reconfirm. If your prospect needs to cancel or postpone your meeting, most will be polite enough to call you or have someone call you on their behalf.

Key action points

- Ensure you do nothing to be rejected personally from now on.

- Do not take rejection of your product or service personally.

- Get a headset.

- Have a mirror on your desk with SMILE written on it.

- Know your 'numbers' and constantly seek to improve on them.

- Design your own results monitor (RM) and use it always.

- Research your prospects and the sector they are operating in.

- Identify all the problems you have been able to solve for prospects and all the opportunities you have been able to expose them to.

- Create questions that help identify the problems and opportunities.

- Remember the 'silent close'.

- Prepare your opening statements and questions.

- Know everything you need to ask and say during your 'conversation'.

- Rehearse how you will handle gatekeepers and voicemail from now on.

- If you are going to use pre-approach letters, use the Killer Sales Formula and the deadly effective, hand-written compliments slip.

- Do not reconfirm appointments.

- Continue with the *GAVA double your sales – fast* process daily.

- Please study and work on applying the techniques in this Master Class for at least one week before moving on.

4

Prospecting for new business 2
Referral prospecting

Fact: Word of mouth recommendations are the only form of advertising that most of us respond to any more.

To illustrate my point, when you last visited a restaurant you had not been to before, did you go because you saw an advertisement for it or because somebody recommended it to you? The last time you went to see a film, was it because you saw an advertisement for it or because somebody told you it was a great film and you really should see it? Of course you may, from time to time, be persuaded by an advertisement or other form of advertising or marketing, but you are most likely to respond on the recommendation of somebody you know and whose judgement you trust.

Referrals are important

I also know that most people in sales ask for referrals, but in my experience it is a very 'hit and miss' affair. Asking for referrals is very rarely built into a salesperson's agenda for a conversation or meeting and is often forgotten in the excitement of making a sale or the disappointment of losing one. From now on I want you to think of referrals in a completely different way. I want you to think of referrals as being at least as important as making a sale and I want you to make asking for them a formal part of every sales presentation. This was a lesson I learned many years ago and very early in my sales career. I had just started working in the financial services sector and during my initial training my sales manager had constantly stressed the importance of obtaining referrals and shown me numerous techniques to achieve that.

I had been struggling for several weeks to make my first sale, and when I had finally achieved that milestone I hurried back to the office to present the completed application form to my sales manager. I remember the scene vividly to this day. I knocked on his door and asked if I might speak to him for a moment. He beckoned me in and I proudly placed the application form on his desk. 'My first sale Bernie,' I said. He removed his glasses, glanced down at the application form, looked up at me and said, 'Well done Bruce; and how many referrals did you get?' Of course, in the excitement of getting my first sale, I had completely forgotten to ask for referrals. Then Bernie taught me a lesson I would never forget. 'Bruce,' he said, 'this application will stay on my desk and will not be processed until you have gone back to the client and obtained at least three referrals.' That is precisely what I had to do, what I did – and what a lesson I learned. That application, which was worth many hundreds of pounds in commission to me, sat on his desk for just over two weeks because the applicants had gone on holiday.

Some years later I developed a referral script for another large insurance company that salespeople are still taught to use some 20 years on. It was based on the concept of including an agreement to get referrals as part of the introduction. It went like this:

I really appreciate the opportunity to meet with you (name) and see how I can be of assistance. May I first of all please just explain the way I work. What I'm going to do is carry out a detailed analysis of your current financial situation and, together with you, define precisely what your financial goals are. I am then going to go away, spend some time putting together a plan which will help you achieve those goals, and then have another

meeting with you to explain my proposals. There is no charge
for that work and therefore I do expect two things in return.
One – that if you like my proposals you will go ahead and place
the business with me and, two – that you will introduce me to at
least three other people in similar circumstances to yourself, with
a strong recommendation from you to them that they meet with
me. Are you OK to go ahead on that basis?

Not one person ever refused to go along with my terms and in
most cases kept to the agreement. That approach of making it a
condition of doing business with me was quite revolutionary in
those days and still works extremely well today. Now we can do
even better.

How to ask for referrals – your referral script

The words you use when asking for referrals are critical, so learn
these well.

When asking for referrals from someone who has not been
referred, you say:

(John), I like to spend my time looking after my customers, not
looking for them, so I would really appreciate your help please.
Who else do you know who might also (be keen to double their
sales – insert your key benefit here) that I should be speaking to
please?'

Now look carefully at the structure of this paragraph:

- '(John)' – people like to hear the sound of their own name.
- 'I like to spend my time looking after my customers, not
  looking for them' – a reason and a benefit for them.
- 'so I would really appreciate your help' – most people do
  genuinely like to help other people.
- 'Please' – one of the three most powerful words in the
  English language. (The others are 'thank you'.)

When the person you are requesting referrals from is a referral themselves, when the script is adapted as follows it becomes even more effective:

> (John), I like to spend my time looking after my customers, not looking for them, so I would really value your help please. (Peter) introduced me to you and several other people and I would really appreciate it if you could do the same please. Who else do you know who might also (be keen to double their sales – insert your key benefit here) that I should be speaking to please?

And if you really want to pack some more punch into it:

> (John), I like to spend my time looking after my customers, not looking for them, so I would really value your help please. (Peter) introduced me to you and seven other people and I would really appreciate it if you could do the same please. Who else do you know who might also (be keen to double their sales – insert your key benefit here) that I should be speaking to please?

You may think this is a little cheeky but if you say it politely and warmly, you will be surprised at how effective this is. Just a few days ago I asked somebody this very question. His response was: 'I'm really sorry Bruce but I don't believe I could think of seven. But I could certainly come up with at least four or five.' 'Thank you very much,' I said.

If you really want to double your sales, learn these scripts off by heart so you never need to think about how you are going to ask for referrals again. I want to be able to wake you up at 2 am from a deep sleep and hear you say those words instantly.

The other psychological technique you should also use when asking for referrals is to have your pen out, poised over a piece of paper, ready to take notes of those referrals and in full view of your customer. When you do this, their conscious mind sees the picture of your pen poised over the paper and connects to something in their subconscious mind associated with that picture, which of course is to supply you with the information you have requested so that you can write it down. You are twice as likely to receive those referrals when you have the pen poised over the paper.

You should also do this when you are requesting referrals over the telephone. The fact that you have the pen poised over the paper connects with associations in your subconscious mind and affects the tone and pitch of your voice and how you speak when you make the request. How you speak also conveys to the other person's subconscious mind that you are holding a pen poised over a piece of paper. Hey presto – referrals as if by magic!

Now, one last thing on this subject of 'how to ask'. When you have got the names and contact details, explain that you do not like to call anyone unannounced and ask them to telephone the referral and make the introduction before you call, or e-mail them and copy you in. Ask them politely to make the call that day. I promise you they will not be in the least bit offended and will comply with your request more often than not. Sometimes, if I think I can squeeze just a little more time out of the meeting, I will even ask them to make the calls while I am there.

" ask them politely to make the call that day "

When to ask for referrals

When I question an audience of salespeople about when they ask for referrals, approximately 70 per cent raise their hands when I ask if they wait until the customer has placed an order with them. Ten per cent confirm they sometimes ask during the sales process if it involves a series of meetings and things are going well. The remaining 20 per cent either do not ask for referrals at all or will not raise their hands, no matter what I ask them.

Not once has anybody who has not heard me speak before ever thought of asking for referrals when they make contact with a potential customer for the first time. Well, now is the time for you to start doing just that. Picture the situation. You have made a cold call to a prospect, you have got on reasonably well and you have made an appointment to go to see them. You have confirmed the date and time and that they have put the information in their diary. Here is what you should now say:

'(Janet), just one last thing. I like to spend my time looking after my customers, not looking for them, so just before I hang up, I would really appreciate your help please. Who else do you know in your area who might also (your key benefit here) that I should be speaking to please? I'd love to make contact with them and arrange to pop in for 15 minutes to introduce myself while I'm there. Who can you think of please?'

If the person you are speaking to is a referral, then of course you adapt what you say as follows:

'(Janet), just one last thing. I like to spend my time looking after my customers, not looking for them, so just before I hang up, I would really appreciate your help please. Peter introduced me to you and several other people and I'd really appreciate it if you could do the same please. Who else do you know in your area who might also (your key benefit here) that I should be speaking to please? I'd love to make contact with them and arrange to pop in for 15 minutes to introduce myself while I'm there. Who can you think of please?'

Some people will give you referrals, some will not. So what? You are no worse off than if you had not asked and I absolutely guarantee you that nobody will ever cancel an appointment they have just made because you asked for referrals before you had even met them. The fact is that in most cases they will admire and respect you for taking such a professional approach to the management of your time and will be looking forward to seeing you even more.

Supposing the person you are speaking to does not want to see you and will not make an appointment. Now what do you do?

The answer is still *ask for referrals*. You have them in a weak moment. Nobody really likes to upset other people and, by turning you down, there is a good chance they are going to be even more likely to want to help you. So you say:

(John), I really appreciate your honesty and not making an appointment with me that would have been a waste of both our time. Just one last thing – I like to spend my time looking after my customers, not looking for them and I would really value your help please. Peter introduced me to you and several other people and I'd really appreciate it if you could do the same please. Who else do you know in your area who might (your key benefit here) that I should be speaking to please?

Once you get into the habit of asking for referrals before you meet and at every meeting, and when you have been turned down, and when you fail to make a sale at a presentation, you will quickly find you are making much more effective use of your time and sales will be increasing substantially. Just to get the point across to you one more time and even more powerfully, I can tell you this as an absolute fact:

Your future income will rise in direct proportion to the number of times you ask the referral questions.

How to encourage even more referrals

Now you have your customers giving you more referrals than you ever had before, how are you going to encourage them to keep giving them to you so you have so much new business coming in that you do not ever have to think of making a cold call again? The answer is to look after that customer, and that means going the extra mile. That extra mile is not a crowded road!

The first and most obvious thing you can do is to look out for potential customers for them. When you are with your customers and other prospective customers, and when you are networking, always be thinking 'which of my customers could be selling to this prospect too?' Whenever you think there is a fit, here is what to say. Look carefully at the way the following paragraph is constructed. It is full of positive statements and potential benefits to your prospect or customer.

Mary, one of the things I also like to do is to help my customers to get more business whenever I can, and I'd like to think I can do the same for you from time to time. Now one of my other customers, (Frank Jessup of ABC Supplies, offers the most fantastic service and prices on stationery). Would you be OK to take a call from him and just explore if there's something you could be doing for each other?

The other thing you can do is to keep your customers updated with new and important information relating to their business sector. You could be picking up this information from a networking group, from the daily newspapers, trade magazines and other sources. I find that by subscribing to Google News Alerts on subjects of interest to my customers, I can get the most up-to-date information delivered to my inbox whenever I wish.

I am not suggesting you deluge your customers with information on a daily or weekly basis. Neither should you e-mail it to them because it will not appear to have great value to them in that format. What you should do, once every three or four weeks, is to print off what you consider to be the three very best articles you have come across. Put these in a neat plastic folder or one of your company's branded folders, hand write a note saying that you thought they might find this information useful, put the package inside an envelope, hand write the address and post it to them or drop by and deliver it by hand. That way it really looks as if you have gone to a lot of trouble on their behalf. The more effort you can put into helping your customers to build their businesses, the more effort they are going to put in to helping you build yours.

❝ it really looks as if you have gone to a lot of trouble ❞

To help summarise what we have covered on the subject of referrals so far, these are my five referral rules:

1 Make giving you referrals a condition of your customers doing business with you.
2 Ask for referrals before you have met the potential customer.
3 Ask for referrals during the meeting with a potential customer.
4 Ask for referrals after meeting with the customer.
5 Encourage ongoing referrals from the customer.

There is one word, other than the word 'referrals', that is common to each of my five referral rules and that word is 'customer'. But what about suppliers? They can be an equally good source of referrals and suppliers have a vested interest in keeping you happy; let's face it – you are spending money with them!

When I first mention this subject in workshops there are some people who seem to have a resistance to it. But these are inevitably the people who have a resistance to asking for referrals in the first place. The other point that is often raised is that their suppliers deal in the business-to-consumer (B2C) market whilst they deal in the business-to-business (B2B) market, or vice versa. But all suppliers have many contacts in both those markets.

A short while ago, I received a telephone call from a salesperson who had attended a Master Class I ran several weeks before. Following my advice and during the following week, she had asked every supplier she spent money with for referrals. She asked the owner of her local corner store where she bought her morning newspaper. She asked the manager in the local DIY shop when she went in to purchase some screws she needed to put up a shelf. She asked her hairdresser when she went to have her hair styled and she asked the local dry cleaner when she went to pick up her clothes. In fact she asked every single person she came into contact with when she was buying from them.

Her approach was very straightforward. She would say: 'I'd really appreciate your help please. I don't know if I have told you this before but I sell security systems for offices and factories. Who do you know within about a 50-mile radius from here who runs a business that works from those type of premises?'

She also asked her sales manager for a list of suppliers the company used and contacted them. Within three weeks she told me that she had received over 75 new referrals and had stopped asking for the moment because she was simply too busy to follow them all up.

So here are an additional five referral rules for you:

1 Make giving you referrals a condition of your suppliers doing business with you. If they won't, change suppliers. Even if it is the corner shop you buy you daily newspaper from.

2 Wherever possible, ask for referrals before you have met the potential supplier.

3 Ask for referrals during the meeting with a supplier.

4 Ask for referrals after meeting with a supplier.

5 Encourage ongoing referrals from a supplier.

Networking

Networking is the only other prospecting technique I want to share with you. It is something that I am sure you are familiar with because networking has become a rapid growth industry in its own right. We have online networking organisations such as Ecademy, Linked In, Twitter and Facebook, to name but a few, which have hundreds of thousands, and in some cases millions of members.

We have offline organisations running face-to-face meetings such as BNI, BRX, the Academy of Chief Executives, and many others, some of which have become worldwide franchise organisations generating millions in income for the franchisees. In spite of that, I often come across people who have attended numerous formal business networking events and have decided that 'networking doesn't work'. The truth of the matter is that networking does work. It is they who have failed to make it work for them. I would therefore like to share some ideas to make it work a lot better for you. I am not however going to talk about online networking; only offline – face to face.

If you have ever been to a formal networking event, then the following scenario may be familiar to you.

A business person, let us call him John, arrives at the networking event venue. There is a large sign over the door which says 'Networking Event' – a final reminder of what John is there for before he enters. Once inside, John looks nervously around at the 40 or 50 people mingling and chatting to each other and finally sees somebody he knows from a previous networking event and heads over to talk to them. After 10 to 15 minutes of idle chatter John decides he has to get on with some real networking and parts company. John then looks around again and sees someone standing alone and obviously feeling uncomfortable, so he goes over to introduce himself. It becomes obvious after just a minute or so that this person is rather boring, has little genuine interest in what John does and probably knows very few people, if any, who would be interested in what John has to offer.

Nevertheless, because John does not want to appear rude and is himself a little nervous with networking, he stays and chats to this gentleman for another 15 minutes before excusing himself. John repeats this 'networking dance' four or five more times during the evening before deciding the event is a waste of time, and leaves with five or six business cards which will almost certainly lay untouched in a drawer for several months before being discarded.

If that scenario is familiar to you because that is how you often conduct yourself at networking events, then stop it! Of course it doesn't work. I'm going to share with you how to network successfully so that you create a network of people who do business with you and, more importantly, constantly refer you to many other people who will do business with you. Before I do that, let us take a look at some networking basics.

First of all, there are two reasons for attending a networking session; the first is to meet people who may want to transact business with you and the second is to meet people who may be able to introduce you to other people who want to do business with you.

Secondly, other successful and well connected people you meet at a networking session are unlikely to remember very much about you the following day.

Thirdly, even if they do remember you, they are unlikely to remember enough about you to telephone you and ask you to discuss doing business and they definitely don't know enough about you to recommend you to other people. It takes most people at least an hour of face-to-face conversation with you before they might start referring you to their contacts, and the more they value their reputation, the longer it may take. You have to prove to them you are referable!

On the basis of those points, you may well ask, 'What's the point of networking then?'

It took me about two years to develop a contact list of over 2000 people I met at networking events before I realised that I was doing something terribly wrong. I finally learned that the purpose of attending a networking event was to meet as many people as possible and to select just a few from the many I met whom I believed were active networkers themselves; who were successful or working hard at becoming successful; that I liked when I first met them; and were people I wanted to spend some time getting to know a lot better and helping them to get to know me a lot better. When you start looking at people and talking to people with that in mind, it soon becomes much easier to identify them at networking events.

Now let us take a look at how John should be working a net-working event.

This time John strides into the room looking positive and at ease. He notices a few people standing alone sipping glasses of wine, looking a little dejected, avoiding eye contact, and ignores them. He then sees a couple of smartly dressed business people talking animatedly and enthusiastically and heads straight towards them. On the way he notices two other people he has met before, one who he has not followed up and another who has become a client. He stops briefly to say a very polite and friendly hello but it is obvious from his manner that he is about to move on quickly, which he does. He approaches the two strangers and stands just a little distance from them, but close enough that he is almost part of the conversation. They of course then notice him, take a brief pause in their conversation and turn to look at him. He then takes his opportunity to speak. 'Hello I'm John Stevens. I couldn't help noticing you both and as we haven't met before, I thought I'd just drop over and introduce myself. I do hope I'm not interrupting.'

Within the space of 15 minutes, John has introduced himself, found out what businesses the other two people are involved with, explained what he does and exchanged business cards with them. He has also decided their rating from one to five; a rating of one being 'not worth following up' and a rating of five being 'definitely worth speaking to again'. He also finds it very easy to extricate himself from this little meeting because he interrupted it in the first place. So he simply says, 'I'm going to leave you gentleman to carry on with what you were discussing before I interrupted you. It was a pleasure to meet you and, if you don't have any objections, I would love to chat with you in the next day or two and see what we might be able to do to help each other. Would that be OK?'

During the next few hours, John joins several other couples and threesomes who are in conversation and by the end of the evening has introduced himself to over 30 people, exchanged business cards with them and has made a note on their cards of their one to five score.

The following day, John goes through those business cards, selects the few people he scored either a four or five and calls each one with a view to meeting for an hour or so to really get to know one another. John has become a power networker.

How you describe what you do – your elevator pitch

Whether you are attending a formal networking meeting, or you just happen to be out for a drink after work with a friend who introduces you to someone they know, or you are at a party or any other event, at some time somebody is going to ask you, 'What do you do?' I hear this question asked of so many people, so many times, and I know it has been asked of them many times before. So I am flabbergasted that most people still struggle to answer the question and are very rarely able to give a brief and exciting description of what they do in a way which makes people want to know more. So this is our next exercise.

I want you to write a brief description of what you, and the business you represent, can do for other people; one which you can be proud of, which excites other people and can be expressed in 10 to 15 seconds. That is known as an *elevator pitch*. Then I want you to write another that would take you a little longer, can be more descriptive and finally a third which can take a little longer still. That last one is the 'tall building' elevator pitch.

Your introductions need to be powerful and based on the WIIFM factor – 'What's In It For Me' the potential customer. It does not necessarily matter what your company's name is unless it's a brand that everyone wants to deal with. It is your name that matters. It is irrelevant if your business was established in 1944. That does not mean you do a great job because you have been around for such a long time. The only thing that matters is that you have something to say which mentions a problem you can solve or an opportunity you can help someone exploit and might inspire the potential customer you are talking to, or someone they know, to find out more about what you can do for them. Here are three examples of my own elevator pitches which illustrate the way they can be constructed.

I'm Bruce King. I help salespeople who are struggling to meet or exceed their targets to increase their sales by at least 50 per cent in just a few weeks.

A slightly longer one:

I'm Bruce King. I help salespeople who are struggling to meet or exceed their targets. I inspire and motivate them and give them techniques to enable them to increase their sales by at least 50 per cent in just a few weeks.

And the tall building version:

I'm Bruce King. I help salespeople who are struggling to meet or exceed their targets. I work with anything from small in-house groups to large conference audiences of a thousand or more. I inspire and motivate them and give them techniques to enable them to increase their sales by at least 50 per cent in just a few weeks. I also have a range of training products available on my website for home study which are equally as effective.

Do you think these might create some interest if the person I was saying them to was either in sales themselves, employed a sales team or organised sales conferences? I can assure you it does.

Let me give you a few more illustrations of how this should be done, using some 'before' and 'after' examples to show you how I adapted other people's 'elevator pitches' to take them from boring to exciting.

Before: I'm John Scott from John Scott Training. I do team building.

After: I'm John Scott. I help fragmented teams align around a common vision to create greater profitability.

Before: I'm a mortgage broker with First National Finance.

After: I'm Kevin Walters. I help first time buyers who are struggling to get financing for the home of their dreams.

Before: I'm Mary McDonnell. I'm with XYZ Medical Equipment. We were established in 1944 and we sell cardiac resuscitation equipment.

After: I'm Mary McDonnell. I sell equipment to medics and para-medics that help to save thousands of lives a year.

Before: I'm John Spiers with Ellingberg CRM Systems. I sell and implement fully integrated CRM systems that are compatible with all major database applications and which are utilised by FT100 companies.

After: I'm John Spiers. I help large organisations manage their customer information to reduce customer turnover and drive repeat sales.

Now create your own elevator pitches for you and your products or services on the following page (Exercise 4.1). When you are really pleased with them, learn them off by heart. I should be able to wake you at 2 am in the morning from a deep sleep and you should be able to repeat your elevator pitches instantly and with enthusiasm. Then whenever anyone asks you, 'What do you do?', you will have that exciting and stimulating answer without having to think about it and lose the moment. You just never know whom you are speaking to and whether what you do may be of interest to them, or someone they know.

exercise 4.1

Your elevator pitches

_____

_____

_____

_____

_____

_____

_____

_____

_____

_____

_____

_____

_____

_____

_____

_____

_____

_____

_____

_____

_____

_____

_____

_____

_____

If you prefer not to write in this book, this form and all others are
available to download at www.bruceking.co.uk/doubleyoursales

Now here is a but – and it is a BIG but...

I have spent some time describing elevator pitches and how to use them. Now I am going to say something you were least expecting. Do not use your elevator pitch when you are networking unless you really have to: in other words, unless someone insists on you telling them what you do. Save your elevator pitch for other situations. Here is why.

When people go to a networking meeting, most want to talk about themselves and do not really have a great interest in being pitched by you. So use this to your advantage. When someone asks you what you do, instead of telling them, say something like: 'Oh it's very boring – tell me what YOU do!'

Of course they will, because that is what they really wanted to do anyway. Now you have the opportunity to ask them questions that will indicate to you whether or not there could be an interest in what you do, the type of people they are connected to and could introduce you to, and a host of other information that will tell you whether or not you want or need to be bothered to tell them what you do when you are eventually asked again.

So after they have given you their elevator pitch, you could ask questions like:

- 'So what's the biggest project you're working on right now?'
- 'Who are you working with on that?'
- 'What help might you need?'
- 'What type of introductions are you seeking?'
- 'Who's your biggest competitor?'

Do you see how, by asking these questions, you can elicit far more information than if you told them what you did and tried to steer the conversation onto how you could help them?

My other networking tip is never to give your business card to somebody at a networking event until you are asked for it. If the person you are speaking to does not offer theirs or ask for yours and it is someone you would like to follow up, say something like:

■ 'I've got some people who you might be interested in talking to you. Give me your card and let's speak in the next couple of days.'

Or

■ 'I've recently written a brief report which might help you with that project. Give me your card and I'll email it to you.'

Then they will almost always ask for your card and because they asked for it, that is the one they will most likely keep and remember you.

My final tip on networking: form your own mastermind group

We have already discussed that there are countless opportunities for networking and I encourage you to attend as many of these as you can and make them work for you. I also encourage you to form your own 'mastermind group'. Here is what you should do.

Your intention should be to form a group of six to eight people at most who commit to meet once every two weeks for a two-hour breakfast session. The purpose of these sessions are three-fold.

1   to exchange market knowledge
2   to introduce potential customers to each other
3   to discuss any particular challenges anyone in the group may be having and advise accordingly.

The people you want in your group should be from companies who are likely to be serving customers in a similar sector to your own but are not in competition with each other. For example, if you sell office furniture, you would be looking to invite sales-people or sales directors who sell carpeting, stationery, computer systems, IT networking solutions, copying equipment, postroom services, office electrical installations, telephone systems, mobile communication solutions, etc.

On Exercise 4.2, put together a list of appropriate organisations in your district and then telephone their sales director, MD or CEO. Explain that you are putting together this mastermind group, the purpose of it, and that you would like to invite them or one of their top salespeople to attend an introductory meeting. You want the best person, not the worst person, and certainly not somebody who is struggling. If you want to double your sales, remember that you want to be flying with the eagles, not twittering with the sparrows!

The purpose of the introductory meeting is to get a commitment from everyone to the three principles and to attend regularly. Then you have your mastermind group.

exercise 4.2

Potential members of my mastermind group

Company	Contact name/position	Telephone no.

If you prefer not to write in this book, this form and all others are available to download at www.bruceking.co.uk/doubleyoursales

Key action points

■ Create and learn your referral scripts.

■ Ask for referrals before you have met a potential customer and every time you meet with them.

■ Ask for referrals from people you fail to secure an appointment with and those you fail to sell to.

■ Keep your eyes open for market information and potential customers for your customers to encourage ongoing referrals.

■ Ask for referrals from your suppliers. If they cannot or will not help, change suppliers.

■ Create and learn your elevator pitches.

■ Form your own mastermind group.

■ Continue with the *GAVA double your sales – fast* process daily.

■ Please study and work on applying the techniques in this Master Class for at least one week before moving on.

5

NLP techniques for salespeople 1
Communication skills that will make people want to buy from you

The goal of effective communication should be for someone to say, 'yes please' rather than 'so what?'
Jim Rohn, business coach and self-help author

Having attended many neuro lingustic programming (NLP) classes myself over the years, it appears to me that a lot of NLP teachers make it seem rather more complicated than it need be. The word 'psychobabble' springs to my mind which, according to the dictionary, is defined as 'writing or talking using jargon from psychiatry or psychotherapy without particular accuracy or relevance'. That is not going to happen here.

Defining NLP and looking at communication

This is my personal definition of NLP, and particularly as it applies to selling more effectively:

NLP is about understanding how we think, how we make decisions and how it affects our behaviour. NLP is about understanding how other people think, how they make decisions and how it affects their behaviour. When we understand how other people think and how they make decisions, we can communicate with them most effectively, in a way they will understand us most clearly and therefore enable us to have the greatest influence over their behaviour.

The most effective communicators are able to create almost instant rapport with people. Everybody likes and trusts them, feels they are understood by them and naturally has a good feeling about them. The best communicators use NLP techniques intuitively. It was by studying such communicators, what they did and how they did it, that led to the understanding that underpins NLP.

There are hundreds of different NLP techniques. For the purpose of this and the following Master Class, I am going to teach you what I consider to be the few most important and effective NLP techniques and how you can use these to help you double your sales – fast.

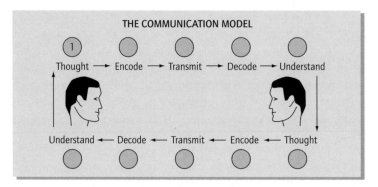

THE COMMUNICATION MODEL

Look at the diagram which illustrates how verbal communication takes place. Starting at point 1 (top left) the first person has a thought. They then encode that; in others words they put their thoughts into words in their mind. They then transmit their words; they speak. The person who they are talking to hears the words and decodes them in a way that they can understand them; has their own thoughts which are then encoded, transmitted, and so the process goes on. If you consider that cycle, then apart from the initial thought (1), the only part of the communication process you can be fairly sure people get right is the transmission. Even then some people do not actually say the words they had intended. So is it any wonder that communication is fraught with difficulty. It is a little like playing Chinese whispers.

Communication is further complicated by the fact that we are not understood solely by the words we use. According to behavioural psychologists, during face-to-face conversation, the words we use account for only 10 per cent of our communication. Thirty-five per cent of communication is how we say those words, and the remaining 55 per cent is how we look when we speak. You should therefore be very aware of how you sound and how your body language matches how you sound, as well as your choice of words.

That, however, is basic communication. NLP goes much deeper than that and, as you will shortly discover, there are many other aspects of the way we communicate that influence those we are communicating with in an attempt to get them to want to buy what we are selling. By learning the techniques in this and the following Master Class you will:

■ establish rapport very quickly

■ understand other people better

■ be understood better

■ influence others far more easily

■ not get upset or frustrated because you will understand how and why other people think differently from you.

Establishing rapport

According to behavioural psychologists, people make a decision on whether they like and trust people within 10 seconds of first meeting or speaking to them. As the meeting continues, we can maintain, and indeed enhance, that rapport or we can destroy it.

The greater the rapport we can establish with a prospect, the more likely we are to sell to them. Therefore, one of the most important things you should want to do is to establish rapport with a prospect as quickly as you possibly can. The faster you can establish rapport, the more likely you are to do business with them.

NLP technique 1 – mirroring

The effectiveness of mirroring as an NLP technique was discovered by behavioural psychologists who noted that when people were getting on very well together, they tended to mirror each other in various ways. They would reflect each other's body language, the way they spoke, their breathing patterns and other traits, and this happened naturally, with no conscious attempt by either person to do so. The psychologists therefore wondered if, by deliberately mirroring another person, that same level of rapport could be created. They tested their theory and found it to be correct.

I mentioned earlier that I was using similar techniques long before NLP was discovered. Very early on in my career, one of my sales managers taught me what he called 'the chameleon technique'; in other words, 'become just like your prospect and you will be far more likely to sell to them'.

The effectiveness of mirroring is based on the fact that most people like to do business with people they like and trust, and the people they most like and trust are people who are most like themselves. They may admire people with different personality traits, mannerisms, ways of speaking and for the way they look, but they feel more comfortable doing business with people who are just like them. Therefore the objective, when you use this technique, is to make the person you are selling to think that they are looking in a mirror and seeing themselves. Mirroring enables you to get in direct contact with your prospect's subconscious mind, and have their subconscious mind say to them: 'This person is just like me. I like them, I trust them and I want to do business with them.' In order to mirror someone effectively, there are three basic things that you can do.

1 Mirror body language

The first mirroring technique is to copy your prospect's body language. In its most basic form and as taught by many NLP practitioners, you mirror your prospect's body language precisely. This is not a technique I recommend but, just to illustrate the technique, we will go along with precise mirroring for the moment. If, for example, you are greeted with a firm handshake, respond with a firm one. If their handshake is weak, yours must also be weak. If your prospect remains standing with a hand in their pocket, you remain standing with a hand in your pocket. If your prospect sits upright, you sit upright. If your prospect sits forward in their chair, you sit forward. If they sit with their arms folded, you sit with your arms folded.

If your prospect crosses their legs, you cross yours too. If they start to fiddle with a pen, tie, piece of paper or anything else, you do the same. Everything you do during the course of your meeting with a prospective client that mirrors their body language will help to establish rapport with that person very quickly. Their subconscious mind will be telling them that they like you, that they trust you and that they would like to do business with you.

Here is an interesting and fun way of testing this technique.

The next time you are going to take a journey on a bus or train, or meeting someone in a hotel foyer for a business meeting, or indeed anywhere where you can sit opposite somebody, make sure you have a book, newspaper or magazine with you. Seat yourself opposite somebody who has a book, newspaper or magazine and start to mirror their activity but avoid making any eye contact. Mirror their body movements. If they cross their legs or uncross them, you do the same. If they scratch their head, their ear or their nose, you do the same. If they fold their newspaper, or turn a page in their magazine or book, you do the same. If they yawn – you yawn. Copy their body movements precisely.

It is almost certain that within a minute or two, they will look across at you with a puzzled look on their face. They will not be thinking 'Why is that person copying me?', they will be thinking 'Where do I know that person from?' Of course they do not know you, but their subconscious mind will be thinking they are seeing themselves – someone just like them!

I mentioned previously that mirroring your prospect's body language precisely is not what I recommend. The reason for this is that mirroring body language precisely is one of the most well-known NLP techniques. It is normally the first thing that is taught and many people who have not even studied NLP are aware of this technique. Mirroring body language therefore needs to be rather more subtle if you don't want to risk being caught out doing it by the other person. If you are caught doing this, then you may well create distrust rather than trust.

Picture the following scene.

You are in a crowded restaurant and sitting a few tables away are a couple who are obviously in love. You cannot hear what they are saying, and assuming they are not actually making love on the table, how do you know they are in love? You know because they are intuitively and subtly mirroring each other and it is so very obvious how well they are getting along together. When one smiles, the other smiles. When one leans forward, so does the other. When one strokes their forehead, the other strokes their chin. When one picks up their wine glass, the other picks up the little flower vase on the table. When one straightens his tie, the other straightens her dress. When one folds their arms, the other crosses their legs. It is still mirroring, but it is a lot more subtle.

Mirroring body language is a very powerful technique for creating immediate rapport. I would just like you to be a little more subtle, as our lovers were when mirroring intuitively. If your prospect has a strong handshake, yours should still also be strong, as it should be weak if theirs is weak. If your prospect remains standing with a hand in their pocket, you can remain standing with a hand in your pocket. There is nothing obvious about that type of mirroring. If your prospect sits upright, you should still sit upright – just wait 10 to 15 seconds before you shift your position. If your prospect sits forward in their chair, you should also sit forward; again just wait 10 to 15 seconds before you shift your position. If they cross their arms, cross your legs instead. If they fiddle with a pen, wait 10 to 15 seconds and then fiddle with a piece of paper or your brochure. If they straighten their tie, straighten your jacket soon after. This type of subtle mirroring is just as effective as precise mirroring and will help you to create the rapport you need – without being caught out doing it.

2 Mirror speech

Have you ever taken a call from someone who was trying to interest you in their company's product or service and, within the space of a few seconds, you found there was something about them that really irritated you and you knew that no matter what they were offering, you were not going to buy it from them? Well the bad news is that you have almost certainly had precisely the same effect on someone else. That is disturbing, is it not?

The reason this happens is that there is something about your voice or their voice that deeply irritates the conscious and the subconscious mind, if for no other reason than it is just different. So the next mirroring technique is to match your prospect's rate, tone and pitch of speech.

If your prospect speaks quickly, then you speak quickly too. If they speak slowly, you speak slowly. If they sound upbeat and excited, you mirror that and sound upbeat and excited. If they sound a little subdued then you sound subdued too. As soon as you have established rapport you can begin to sound a little more upbeat and they will become upbeat and more positive too. If they have a deep voice, lower the pitch of your voice to match it. If they have a higher pitched voice, raise the pitch of yours a little also. By mirroring your prospect's rate, tone and pitch of speech you are sending a message to their subconscious mind that you are just like them and it is OK for them to like you, trust you and do business with you.

> **" your message is that you are just like them and it is OK for them to like you "**

3 Mirror breathing

The other mirroring technique you should use is to mirror your prospect's breathing pattern. This is a most powerful technique for establishing rapport at a very deep subconscious level. It takes a little more practise, but it is worth the extra time it takes to become really good at this. The easiest way to do this is to realise that if someone is speaking, they cannot be breathing in at the same time. So when they are speaking – you breathe out. When they pause for breath, you too breathe in – and so on.

There are two other mirroring techniques you can use, which are not necessarily as important but can also have an impact on the effectiveness of establishing rapport with your prospect. These are to mirror what they wear and what they eat.

Mirror what they wear

With regards to what they wear, I am not suggesting that you should be silly enough to start dressing as somebody of the opposite sex or copying precisely what you know they are likely to be wearing so you look like twins. However, I do want you to be conscious of not being overdressed or underdressed. For example, I recently taught this technique to a salesperson who was struggling to meet his targets selling animal feed to farmers, as indeed were most of his colleagues. He tried out my suggestion of swapping his designer raincoat and smart leather shoes for a green Barbour mackintosh and Wellington boots. His sales increased by 30 per cent just by this change in his dress code. Neither did he have to spend hours scraping the mud off his shoes and polishing them every day.

Another, who sold into the record industry, had always dressed like a city gent. He was very smart and conventionally dressed and looked rather out of place in a meeting of trendy entertainment executives who never wore ties. Although he was slightly older than many of his prospects, getting him to dress a little more like them with a designer suit and very smart, but trendy, shirts without a tie, enabled him to increase his sales by 23 per cent in a matter of a few months.

Mirror what they eat

How about mirroring what prospects eat? If you are offered tea or coffee, if you can bear to do so, choose what your prospect chooses. The fact that you are drinking the same beverage as your prospect will help to reinforce in their subconscious mind that you are similar to them and that they like you, trust you and can do business with you.

I explained this technique to a book publisher one morning. She was very concerned about a lunch meeting she was having with a buyer from a major department store. In the past, he had always been very difficult to get on with and was reluctant to place more than just a small order with her.

The publisher called me back later that day. She told me that she had tried, but found it very difficult to copy the buyer's body language and the way they spoke. She had, however, not found it difficult to order the same food and drink as her prospect. Apparently, by the time the dessert trolley came around and she ordered the strawberries and cream, as her prospect had, he was, in her own words, 'virtually eating out of my hand'. She came away with the biggest order she had ever received from that buyer and, in addition, developed a completely different relationship with him that, over the next few years, made her a great deal of money.

By mirroring your prospect's style of dress and what they eat and drink, you are sending a message to their subconscious mind that you are just like them and it is OK for them to like you, trust you and do business with you.

NLP technique 2 – matching communication modes

Have you ever gone to a meeting where you had sussed out the prospect thoroughly, you knew your product would be immensely useful to them, that they had the money and the authority to buy and you were convinced they would – and yet they did not and you could not fathom out why they turned you down? You may be about to find out the reason why they said 'no'.

There are three main ways in which we think, speak and understand. NLP teachers often refer to these as representational systems. I prefer to use the term 'communication modes'. The following are the main communication modes. We all use all three of these communication modes throughout the day, often switching from one to another depending upon different circumstances. However, most of us have one which is more dominant than the other and which we use particularly when we are making important decisions, such as deciding to buy something. These are the three.

1 Visual

Visual communication means that we think, understand and communicate with ourselves and others through pictures. Another way of putting this is that we 'see' our world. When we are thinking things through, we create pictures in our conscious minds. When we read words or hear words being said to us, we translate those words into pictures in our minds to fully understand them.

2 Auditory

Auditory communication means that we think, understand and communicate with ourselves and others through sounds. Another way of putting this is that we 'hear' our world. When we are thinking things through, we run the words through our conscious minds and talk to ourselves. If we see a picture, we translate that into words and sounds in our minds to fully understand it.

3 Kinaesthetic

Kinaesthetic communication means that we think, understand and communicate with ourselves and others though our feelings. Another way of putting this is that we 'feel' our world. When we are thinking things through, we rely on how we feel about the situation in order to make our decisions.

As I said earlier, most of us have one communication mode which is most dominant, so before we move on to how we use this knowledge let's find out which is your dominant communication mode. Complete the questionnaire in Exercise 5.1 (overleaf). There are 15 sections and you need to select the one response that most appeals to you in each numbered section. Do this as quickly as possible because the faster you respond to the questions, the more accurate the results will be. When you have completed all 15, total the number of A, B and C responses.

Which is your dominant communication mode?

For each question tick only one of A, B or C.

1 A ❐ I love to listen to music.

   B ❐ I enjoy art galleries and window shopping.

   C ❐ I feel compelled to dance to good music.

2 A ❐ I would rather take an oral test than a written test.

   B ❐ I was good at spelling in school.

   C ❐ I tend to answer questions using my gut feeling.

3 A ❐ I've been told I have a good speaking voice.

   B ❐ My confidence increases when I look good.

   C ❐ I enjoy being touched.

4 A ❐ I can resolve problems more quickly when I talk out loud.

   B ❐ I would rather be shown an illustration than have something explained to me.

   C ❐ I find myself holding or touching things as they are being explained.

5 A ❐ I can usually tell someone's sincerity from the tone of their voice.

   B ❐ I find myself evaluating people based on their appearance.

   C ❐ The way others shake hands means a lot to me.

6 A ❐ I would rather listen to cassettes than read books.

   B ❐ I like to watch TV and go to the movies.

   C ❐ I like hiking and other outdoor activities.

7 A ❐ I can hear the slightest noise that my car makes.

   B ❐ It's important that my car is clean inside and out.

   C ❐ I like a car that feels good when I drive it.

8 A ❐ Others tell me that I'm easy to talk to.

   B ❐ I enjoy 'people watching'.

   C ❐ I often touch people when talking to them.

9 A ❐ I am very conscious of what voices sound like on the telephone as well as face to face.

   B ❐ I often remember what someone looked like but forget their name.

C ❏ I can't remember what people look like.

10 A ❏ I often find myself humming or singing to the radio.

B ❏ I enjoy photography.

C ❏ I like to make things with my hands.

11 A ❏ I would rather have an idea explained to me than read about it.

B ❏ I enjoy speakers more if they use visual aids.

C ❏ I like to participate in activities rather than watch.

12 A ❏ I am a good listener.

B ❏ I picture how someone looks when I am speaking to them on the telephone.

C ❏ I feel positive or negative toward others, sometimes without knowing why.

13 A ❏ I sometimes speak out loud when I am thinking.

B ❏ I am good at finding my way using a map.

C ❏ I exercise because of the way I feel afterwards.

14 A ❏ I like a house with rooms that allow for quiet areas.

B ❏ It's important that my house is clean and tidy.

C ❏ I like a house that feels comfortable.

15 A ❏ I like to try to imitate the way people talk.

B ❏ I make a list of things I need to do each day.

C ❏ I've been told that I'm well coordinated.

Count the total number of A responses, B responses and C responses and note these below.

A RESPONSES ☐   B RESPONSES ☐   C RESPONSES ☐

If you have more A responses your dominant communication mode is auditory.

If you have more B responses your dominant communication mode is visual.

If you have more C responses your dominant communication mode is kinaesthetic.

If you prefer not to write in this book, this questionnaire is available to complete online at www.bruceking.co.uk/doubleyoursales

Determining their communication mode

A communication mode is, to some extent, a language in which your prospect thinks, understands, and makes decisions. Therefore if you can define which communication mode is dominant in your prospect and can speak to them in that same language, you are far more likely to be fully understood and obtain a buying decision. So how do you determine your prospect's dominant communication mode? This is far easier than you might first imagine. You simply ask questions as you would normally do and listen carefully for the words and phrases that your prospect uses in their response to you.

Prospects who are predominantly **visual** will use words and phrases such as:

'I don't *see* what you mean.'

'I hadn't *pictured* it quite like that.'

'I can *see* your point of view.'

'I need to *focus* on the bottom line.'

'It *appears* to me.'

'*Imagine* the situation.'

'That's my *perspective* on that.'

'I have a *hazy* idea of what they mean.'

'Let's not make a *scene*.'

'He took a *dim view* of that.'

'I have a *mental image*.'

'Can you *visualise* this?'

Are you beginning to *see* how easy this is?

Prospects who are predominantly **auditory** will use words and phrases such as:

'That *sounds* expensive.'

'I haven't *heard* about that.'

'That *rings* a bell.' (or '*rings* true')

'I *hear* what you are *saying*.'

'I wouldn't *say* that.'

'*Explain* it to me.'

'You're not *listening.*'

'How would you *define* that?'

'That's *music* to my ears.'

'Got that *loud* and clear.'

'Give me an *account* of…'

'He's a *blabbermouth.*'

Does this *sound* as if it is going to be easy for you to learn to do?

Prospects who are predominantly **kinaesthetic** will use words and phrases such as:

'I don't *feel* it's for us.'

'I think we can *firm up* an agreement.'

'My *gut* feeling tells me.'

'I'm not *comfortable* with that.'

'We've been having a *rough* time.'

'Get a *handle* on this.'

'Get in *touch* with.'

'We're *under pressure* to perform.'

'I *love* that idea.'

'She's *cool, calm and collected.*'

'Let's *pull out* all the stops.'

'Those will be *firm* foundations.'

Now do you *feel* you could pick this up easily?

Once you have established your prospect's dominant communication mode, here is how you adapt what you say and your presentation to communicate with them in the most effective way.

Communicating with a visual

If someone is dominantly visual, it is important to realise they are very strong on first impressions and things need to 'look right'. That includes you and how you present yourself.

Visually dominant people love to see diagrams, photographs and pictures and tend to look at the 'big picture' rather than the small details. They tend to be very quick thinkers, so keep your presentation going at a good pace.

When a visual dominant person asks you a question or makes a statement and uses a visual word or phrase, you repeat it back to them and use other words that match their dominant communication mode. For example, if a prospect were to say to you 'I hadn't pictured it working quite like that', you would say 'I *see* you hadn't *pictured* it working quite like that, so may I *show* you how this works and could solve that problem we discussed earlier?'

Communicating with an auditory

If someone is dominantly auditory, it is particularly important to mirror their rate, tone and pitch of speech and be very precise with your choice of words. Avoid presenting to them in noisy environments where they are likely to be distracted by sounds.

When they ask you a question or make a statement and use an auditory word or phrase, you simply repeat it back to them and use other words that match their dominant communication mode. For example, if a prospect were to say to you 'That *sounds* expensive', you would say 'I appreciate that *sounds* expensive Mrs Prospect, so may I just *talk* you through all the additional features that account for that price difference?'

If you need to use brochures, pictures, charts or any other form of visual support to illustrate your points, be very careful not to just pass that information across to them to look at. I am sure that at some time when you have offered a prospect a chart or diagram, you have either seen a look of disinterest or they have brushed them aside and asked you just to explain your point. An auditory person needs to hear your information in words – not pictures. So talk them through what you are showing them.

Communicating with a kinaesthetic

If someone is dominantly kinaesthetic, they love touching and using things and respond particularly well when you are demonstrative and emotional about your product or service. For a kinaesthetic to make a decision to go with your recommendations, it has to feel right to them. They are the classic 'gut feeling' decision makers.

Just as with the other two dominant communication modes, when a kinaesthetic asks you a question or makes a statement and uses a kinaesthetic word or phrase, you repeat it back to them and use other words that match their dominant communication mode. For example, if a prospect were to say to you 'I don't feel that would work for us', you would say 'I understand you don't *feel* it would work for you. Would you allow me to lend you a demo model so you can *use* it and get a proper *feel* for how this could help you? I'm sure you will *love* it when you do.'

A final tip

At first read, matching communication modes may seem a rather more complex technique than any that we have covered so far in these Master Classes. The easiest way to learn how to do this is to work on identifying and responding to just one of the three dominant modes to start with. Once you have got used to doing that and are comfortable with it, which usually takes a few days, you then start identifying and responding to a second dominant mode simultaneously. When you are comfortable working with both of those, then start identifying and responding to the third. Rest assured that once you start practising this, you will find it quite easy.

As well as doing this with your business prospects, practise whenever else you get the opportunity. If you are socialising with colleagues and friends, sit back and listen rather than speak all the time. Identify their dominant communication mode. If there is a television programme which is an unscripted debate or other unscripted programme, watch it and listen to what the panel are saying and identify each of their dominant communication modes. If there is an interview with someone on a radio programme, listen to that. Once you get into the habit of doing this it will become much easier to identify a dominant communication mode and the more you do it, the more successful you will become at influencing people.

When you speak your prospect's language and communicate with them in their dominant communication mode, they will understand you and the benefits of your proposals far better and be more likely to do business with you.

When you match your prospect's dominant communication mode, you will also be mirroring them and sending a very strong message to their subconscious mind that you are just like them and it is OK for them to like you, trust you and do business with you.

Key action points

- As well as your choice of words, be aware of how you sound and how your body language matches how you sound and your choice of words.

- Subtly mirror your prospect's body language.

- Mirror your prospect's rate, tone and pitch of speech.

- Mirror your prospect's breathing.

- Identify and communicate with your prospects in their dominant communication mode. Practise identifying dominant communication modes at every opportunity.

- Continue with the *GAVA double your sales – fast* process daily.

- Please study and work on applying the techniques in this Master Class for at least one week before moving on.

6

NLP techniques for salespeople 2

Advanced communication skills that will make people want to buy from you even more

The problem with communication is the illusion that it has been accomplished.

George Bernard Shaw, Irish playwright and Nobel Prize winner

I n this Master Class I am going to teach you a rather more advanced NLP technique and a system for using it which will make it relatively easy for you to put it into practice. In fact, you will be sitting an exam at the end of this Master Class and I'm very confident you will pass with flying colours. Just please take your time when going through the following information; there is much to learn, so do take it step by step.

NLP teachers usually describe the technique you are about to study as 'identifying meta programs' and they define meta programs as 'unconscious, content free programs we run in our minds to filter experiences'.

As you will have gathered by now, I like to keep subject titles simple and definitions easy to understand. I call this technique 'strategy filters' and my explanation of this technique is as follows:

It is the subconscious strategy we go through when we make decisions, based on all of our previous experiences. We put the information we receive and the information we have stored, through one or more of several filters in our brain that we have subconsciously decided to use, and make our decisions with those filters.

If we do not understand which filters our prospect is using to make a decision, we are in danger of clashing with them if we are using a different filter from them when asking questions and presenting our proposals. When we are able to determine which filters our prospect is using to make their decision, and use the same filter, we can understand them better, be understood better and have a much stronger influence over their decision-making process. Because you will understand how and why they think differently from you, neither will you get upset or frustrated.

Although most people only use two or three filters, there are a total of five filters we could be using. These are:

1 The similarity or difference filter
2 The self or others filter
3 The away from or towards filter
4 The detail or big picture filter
5 The process or options filter.

In order to fully understand these filters, and how we can use them to sell more effectively, I shall now take you through a series of exercises and examples.

The similarity or difference filter

SIMILARITY ☐   DIFFERENCE ☐

Look at the picture opposite and write in the space below it or on a separate sheet, what the relationship between these figures is or what first came into your mind.

Maybe you wrote something like:

■ they are all arrows, or

■ they are arrows pointing upwards, or

■ they form or are part of a pattern, or

■ there is an arrow missing.

If you did, you are most likely to be filtering information at the *similarity* end of the *similarity or difference* filter.

SIMILARITY ☑   DIFFERENCE ☐

Alternatively, you may have written something like:

■ two arrows are leaning towards each other and one is leaning away, or

■ two arrows are parallel to each other and one is not

■ there is a larger space between the bottom of the first two than the second and third.

If you did, you are most likely to be filtering information at the *difference* end of the *similarity or difference* filter.

SIMILARITY ☐   DIFFERENCE ☑

If you identify your prospect is thinking with a *similarity or difference* filter, you need to know which end of the filter they are using so that you can communicate with them in the way they like to filter information.

Prospects who filter information at the *similarity* end of the *similarity or difference* filter will say things like:

■ 'I've seen this pattern before.'

- 'Who else is using this approach?'
- 'It's another way of...'

They are looking for *similarities*.

Prospects who filter information at the *difference* end of the *similarity or difference* filter will say things like:

- 'But everyone's doing that; we need to be different.'
- 'How do we get across that we do it better?'
- 'Ours is less expensive to run.'

They are looking for ways to *differentiate* themselves.

When you are selling to someone you know is filtering at the *similarity* end of this filter, you should make statements and ask questions like:

- 'Can you see how this is just a greatly improved version of our XYZ Model?'
- 'Most other businesses we deal with have upgraded to this.'
- 'It's the same approach but will take a lot less of your time.'

When you are selling to someone you know is filtering at the *difference* end of this filter, you should make statements and ask questions like:

- 'This will really differentiate you from the competition.'
- 'It would be great to be the first to be doing it this way, wouldn't it?'
- 'This is so different from anything your customers will have seen before.'

The self or others filter

SELF ☐   OTHERS ☐

How do you know when you have done a good job? Write your answer in the space below or on a separate sheet, before continuing.

Maybe you wrote something like:

- I just know when I have, or
- I feel great about myself, or
- I see my sales figures are over target.

If you did, you are most likely to be filtering information at the *self* end of the *self or others* filter.

SELF ☑   OTHERS ☐

Alternatively, you may have written something like:

- I get great feedback from my customers, or
- The boss congratulates me in front of the team, or
- Everyone in the office tells me I've done a great job.

If you did, you are most likely to be filtering information at the *others* end of the *self or others* filter.

SELF ☐   OTHERS ☑

If you identify your prospect is thinking with a *self or others* filter, you need to know which end of the filter they are using so that you can communicate with them in the way they like to filter information.

Prospects who filter information at the *self* end of the *self or others* filter will say things like:

- 'It feels wrong (or right) to me.'
- 'I need to be convinced.'
- 'This is what I want to see.'

They are focused on how *they* feel about something.

Prospects who filter information at the *others* end of the *self or others* filter will say things like:

- 'How has this worked for others before?'

- 'This will win them over.'
- 'You don't understand what we need.'

They are focused on what *others* feel about something.

When you are selling to someone you know is filtering at the *self* end of this filter, you should make statements and ask questions like:

- 'What do you need to see?'
- 'You need to feel really comfortable with this.'
- 'You need to see this working first.'

When you are *selling* to someone you know is filtering at the *others* end of this filter, you should make statements like:

- 'This is where it has worked best elsewhere.'
- 'Your customers will love the fact you're introducing this service.'
- 'Everyone we've shown this to is amazed at the improved performance.'

The away from or towards filter

AWAY FROM ☐   TOWARDS ☐

Imagine you are in the market for a new piece of office equipment. There are only two things available for you to base your decision on and you can *only* have one of them. The first is a glossy sales brochure containing lots of features and benefits and lovely photographs. The other is a case study describing the problems the company was able to solve for another organisation using this equipment. Which one will you choose? Write your answer in the space below or on a separate sheet.

_____

_____

If you chose the case study, you are most likely to be filtering information at the *away from* end of the *away from or towards* filter.

AWAY FROM ☑   TOWARDS ☐

If you chose the glossy sales brochure, you are most likely to be filtering information at the *towards* end of the *away from or towards* filter.

AWAY FROM ☐   TOWARDS ☑

If you identify your prospect is thinking with an *away from or towards* filter, you need to know which end of the filter they are using so that you can communicate with them in the way they like to filter information.

Prospects who filter information at the *away from* end of the *away from or towards* filter will say things like:

■ 'Will this cause problems in the admin department?'

■ 'If we can fix this, they won't go elsewhere, will they?'

■ 'How can you help us solve this problem?'

They are focused on *avoiding and solving problems*.

Prospects who filter information at the *towards* end of the *away from or towards* filter will say things like:

■ 'We can really change things for the better here.'

■ 'This is an opportunity to show our customers how much better our service is.'

■ 'Will this help us get ahead of our competition?'

They are focused on *exploiting opportunities*.

When you are selling to someone you know is filtering at the *away from* end of this filter, you should make statements and ask questions like:

■ 'These are the three problems this will solve for you.'

■ 'This will help you fix things fast so you can move on.'

■ 'What challenges would you like to get out of the way first?'

When you are selling to someone you know is filtering at the *towards* end of this filter, you should make statements and ask questions like:

- 'This is a great opportunity for you to change things for the better.'
- 'These are the three main benefits you will achieve as a result.'
- 'What would it mean to you if you could get an additional 10 per cent market share?'

The detail or big picture filter

DETAIL ☐   BIG PICTURE ☐

In the space below, or on a separate sheet, write down a little about your home.

_____

_____

_____

_____

_____

If you wrote down a lot of detail such as the precise location, the style of the house, when it was built and by whom, the number of bedrooms, bathrooms, living rooms, the size of the rooms, if it has a conservatory, a single or double garage, a carriage drive, any mention of colour schemes etc., you are most likely to be filtering information at the *detail* end of the *detail or big picture* filter.

DETAIL ☑   BIG PICTURE ☐

If you wrote down a simple statement such as 'it's a big, old, four-bedroom house with a barn in the Hertfordshire countryside', you are most likely to be filtering information at the *big picture* end of the *detail or big picture* filter.

DETAIL ☐   BIG PICTURE ☑

If you identify your prospect is thinking with a *detail or big picture* filter, you need to know which end of the filter they are using so that you can communicate with them in the way they like to filter information.

Prospects who filter information at the *detail* end of the *detail or big picture* filter will say things like:

■ 'I need to understand every single aspect of this, so give me the full specification to study.'

■ 'I need to examine every aspect of your proposed solution.'

■ 'Precisely how much time will we need to allocate to training before we start seeing an increase in sales?'

They are focused on *details*.

Prospects who filter information at the *big picture* end of the *detail or big picture* filter will say things like:

■ 'Just give me the bottom line.'

■ 'Never mind the detail – what's it going to do for us overall?'

■ 'What's it about – in a nutshell?'

They are focused on *the big picture*.

When you are selling to someone you know is filtering at the *detail* end of this filter, you should make statements and ask questions like:

■ 'Can I give you some more detail and a sample to inspect?'

■ 'How much more information do you need?'

■ 'These comply to British Standard Number XXX. Do you need to see a copy of the BS Standard?'

When you are selling to someone you know is filtering at the *big picture* end of this filter, you should make statements and ask questions like:

■ 'Let's look at the big picture.'

■ 'Shall I summarise the major benefits first?'

■ 'The ultimate intention is to...'

The process or options filter

PROCESS ☐   OPTIONS ☐

> In the space below, or on a separate sheet, write down how you chose your current car or job.

_____

_____

_____

_____

> If you wrote down all the stages in your thinking process, a more or less step-by-step process of how you came to your decision; such as first we did this, then we did that, then we evaluated this etc., you are most likely to be filtering information at the _process_ end of the _process or options_ filter.

PROCESS ☑   OPTIONS ☐

> If you wrote down a simple statement such as 'I chose this car because it would cope with just about anything we'd want to use it for' or 'I wanted this job because there were lots of options for switching roles and likely promotions in the future', you are most likely to be filtering information at the _option_ end of the _process or option_ filter.

PROCESS ☐   OPTIONS ☑

> If you identify your prospect is thinking with a _process or options_ filter, you need to know which end of the filter they are using so that you can communicate with them in the way they like to filter information.

> Prospects who filter information at the _process_ end of the _process or options_ filter will say things like:

> ■ 'I need to understand every step of the process.'
> ■ 'Explain to me each stage of this training programme.'

■ 'We have had five new initiatives this month and I'm still writing the manuals for the team so they fully understand the process.'

They are focused on the *process*.

Prospects who filter information at the *options* end of the *process or options* filter will say things like:

■ 'We're locked into old processes and can't respond to changes fast enough.'

■ 'Can we keep our options open on this?'

■ 'What other ways are there of doing this?'

They are focused on having *options*.

When you are selling to someone you know who is filtering at the *process* end of this filter, you should make statements and ask questions like:

■ 'What is your precise decision-making process?'

■ 'How would you like us to implement this system?'

■ 'We'll take you through the process step by step so you fully understand all of the benefits.'

When you are selling to someone you know who is filtering at the *options* end of this filter, you should make statements and ask questions like:

■ 'There are a number of options to choose from.'

■ 'You won't be restricted in how you can develop the program later.'

■ 'There are lots of different add-ons and extras available when you need them.'

Some extra help

There was quite a lot of information for you to take in throughout this and the previous Master Class. You may therefore be thinking this subject is a little complicated and is going to need a great deal more study before you can use this information effectively. I believe that when you take the following tests, you will realise you have already learned much more than you thought. With just a little more practice, you will soon become expert at identifying your prospect's dominant communication modes and their filtering systems and learn to respond effectively very quickly indeed.

In order to help you do this, I designed a simple little tool you can use that keeps you aware of what you need to be looking out for when having a conversation with a prospect, either face to face or on the telephone. I call it my calibration label. Below is an example of the label and if you would like to go to my website at www.bruceking.co.uk/doubleyoursales you can download the artwork which can be printed direct on to a self-adhesive label sheet.

I stick these labels in my day book, my diary, on my notepads, mind maps and anything else I might use when speaking to a client. It reminds me to take the trouble to analyse them before I start to make any comments or suggestions in a way they might not fully understand. I simply tick the relevant box when I have identified them as visual, auditory or kinaesthetic and when I notice any of the filters they are using.

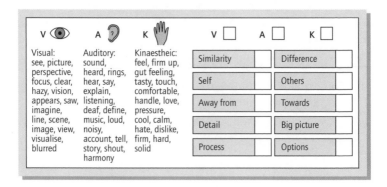

Putting it all together

Now I will show you a few examples of how to calibrate your prospect and how to present your response when you have done so.

Example 1

Prospect: 'I hadn't pictured it quite like that. We do need to stand out from our competitors but we have a lot of other problems to deal with right now before we can move forward.'

Here is my calibration label for this prospect:

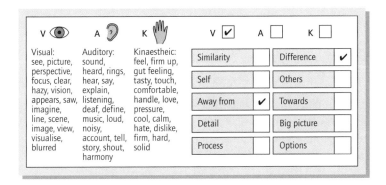

Response: 'I see you hadn't pictured it quite like that Mr Prospect. The solution you have seen is not being used by anyone else in your industry right now and because of the other features I showed you, it's going to solve those three problems you illustrated which have been holding you back until now.'

Example 2

Prospect: 'My gut feeling tells me this could work out well. It's obviously a better version of the model we're currently using and I just need to get comfortable with the installation process and make sure we fully understand it.'

Here is my calibration label for this prospect:

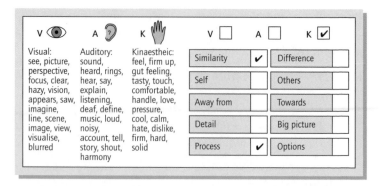

Response: 'I'm really delighted you are comfortable with this Mrs Prospect. It's very similar to your current model in many ways and at the same time, there's been some tremendous improvements in its flexibility on the production line. What I'll do is arrange a demonstration so you can get a good feel for it and I'll have my technical team put together a detailed manual showing you precisely the process for installing it and taking advantage of those additional features.'

Example 3

Prospect: 'Sounds OK so far. Of course I've got to be totally satisfied it will do what you have said. What else is this going to do to help me achieve my goals, and what options will we have to build on this in the future?

Here is my calibration label for this prospect:

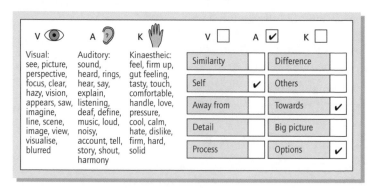

Response: 'I appreciate you telling me it sounds good so far Mr Prospect and of course you should only go ahead when you are totally satisfied. The five major benefits you'll get when you do are..., and there will be plenty of other options to capitalise on this in the future as we introduce more variations.'

Your exam

Note: This exam can also be completed online at www.bruceking.co.uk/doubleyoursales.

Study the statements below and complete the calibration label for each of these prospects. The answers appear at the end of the chapter.

1   I feel this is a similar situation to the one we had with our dealer in Manchester. We all did a fabulous job of boosting sales there and they really loved us for that. The opportunity is 10 times greater.

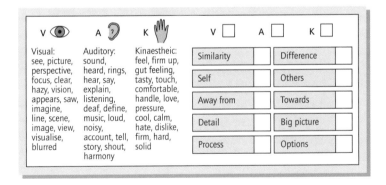

V ◉	A 👂	K ✋	V ☐	A ☐	K ☐
Visual: see, picture, perspective, focus, clear, hazy, vision, appears, saw, imagine, line, scene, image, view, visualise, blurred	Auditory: sound, heard, rings, hear, say, explain, listening, deaf, define, music, loud, noisy, account, tell, story, shout, harmony	Kinaestheic: feel, firm up, gut feeling, tasty, touch, comfortable, handle, love, pressure, cool, calm, hate, dislike, firm, hard, solid	Similarity ☐ Self ☐ Away from ☐ Detail ☐ Process ☐		Difference ☐ Others ☐ Towards ☐ Big picture ☐ Options ☐

2   I recently heard some news about our main competitor. We don't want to carry on doing things the same way as them; everyone I've spoken to says their approach is old fashioned. This is an opportunity for us to show we are really different from the competition.

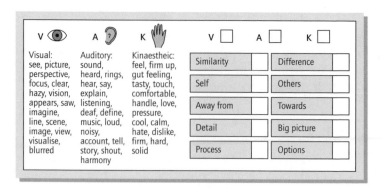

3 I could possibly see this working for us. If I look at the big picture, I could visualise us being number one in our field if this works. But I have to make sure I can avoid any potential problems with the board of directors.

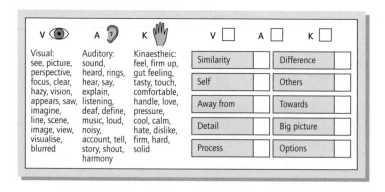

4 I just hate it that so many enquiries don't get put through to our sales team fast enough. It makes us all feel very uncomfortable. We need you to tell us what CRM systems others are using in our industry so we can grab every opportunity to make more sales. Then we need to understand the step-by-step process for integrating a new system with our current switchboard.

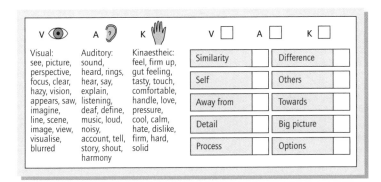

5   That doesn't look good to me. I couldn't possible see myself recommending it to my colleagues on the basis of what you have shown me so far. We have enough problems to fix right now and I just don't need any more to have to watch over.

V 👁	A 👂	K ✋
Visual:	Auditory:	Kinaestheic:
see, picture,	sound,	feel, firm up,
perspective,	heard, rings,	gut feeling,
focus, clear,	hear, say,	tasty, touch,
hazy, vision,	explain,	comfortable,
appears, saw,	listening,	handle, love,
imagine,	deaf, define,	pressure,
line, scene,	music, loud,	cool, calm,
image, view,	noisy,	hate, dislike,
visualise,	account, tell,	firm, hard,
blurred	story, shout,	solid
	harmony	

V ☐	A ☐	K ☐
Similarity		Difference
Self		Others
Away from		Towards
Detail		Big picture
Process		Options

Key action points

■ Download the calibration label artwork at
www.bruceking.co.uk/doubleyoursales.

■ Stick labels in your day book, diary, notepads, mind maps and
anything else you might use when speaking or listening to
anyone. Tick the relevant box when you have identified the
person as visual, auditory or kinaesthetic and when you notice
any of the filters they are using. Practise at every opportunity.

■ Identify and communicate with your prospects in their
dominant communication mode and using their filters. Use the
calibration labels when speaking to them.

■ Continue with the *GAVA double your sales – fast* process daily.

■ Please study and work on applying the techniques in this
Master Class for at least one week before moving on.

Answers

1: Kinaesthetic	2: Auditory	3: Visual
Similarity	Difference	Big picture
Others	Others	Away from
Towards	Towards	

4: Kinaesthetic	5: Visual
Others	Self
Towards	Away from
Detail	

How did you do on that exam? If you got three or more out of
the five correct, then considering you have only just studied this
material, you are doing very well indeed. Go over this Master
Class again several times, put what you learn into practice
regularly and, within no time at all, you will be an expert.

7

The ultimate selling system
Putting *you* in control of the sales process

The most important thing is not which system you use. The
most important thing is you have a system.
Zig Ziglar, self-help author and motivational speaker

If you do not have a selling system that puts you in control,
then you are going to default to the buyer's 'buying system' and
they are going to be in control. Which would you prefer?

Yes, buyers do have a system. Some buyers have developed
their own system and others have been trained how to buy.
In fact, many buyers for larger corporations have more
training in buying and negotiating than salespeople have in
selling. However, I am not referring to formal buying procedures
here; I am referring to five fundamental traits that many
prospects you want to sell to have in common. These are:

1   They know that a salesperson is meeting them with the
    intention of selling to them and are therefore immediately
    defensive, even if they are a referral.

2   They think their time is more valuable than your time and
    do not, or will not, think twice about cancelling an
    appointment at the last moment. Worse still, they just don't
    show up!

3   They believe it is perfectly all right to lie to you and mislead
    you. Prospects who are generally totally honest and always

act with integrity in almost every other situation, will have no qualms about not telling the truth to salespeople.

4 They want to know what you know about the sector you are working in. They may ask for information about your customers and their competition and they want to know everything about your product and service and what it is you are doing for others. It is called unpaid consulting.

5 Having spent a considerable amount of time carrying out your unpaid consulting and sometimes producing complex reports and suggestions, they then think it is perfectly all right to ignore any of your follow-up calls or other forms of correspondence. They will however, most graciously, give you unlimited access to their PA or voicemail.

The 10-step system

Unless you have a selling system that overcomes most, if not all of these traits, you are going to find it much harder to sell to them. The system I am about to teach you is one I have been using and refining for many years. It breaks down into 10 steps:

1 Your initial contact
2 Establish rapport
3 Agree an agenda
4 Get an up-front agreement to your terms
5 Establish authority and, if a complex sale, the buying process
6 Ask 'facts questions'
7 Ask 'issue questions'
8 Present your features and benefits
9 Negotiate and handle objections
10 Close the sale

Irrespective of whether you are selling a product or service which can be sold at the first meeting, or one that involves a complex sale with a long selling cycle, these same steps will usually apply.

The fundamental difference in a complex sale will be that some steps may be weeks or months apart and may involve presentations to several people who may be involved in the decision-making process.

This Master Class will deal with the first eight steps; the last two will be dealt with in the following Master Classes.

Your initial contact

The approach for your initial contact has been covered in detail in Master Class 3 and Master Class 4.

Establish rapport

Establishing rapport has been covered in detail in Master Class 5. The main point I would like you to remember is that it is important to establish rapport at the beginning of every meeting with a prospect, no matter how many times you have met before. Your prospect's attitude to you may have changed, their usual mood may be affected due to personal or business circumstances, or they may simply have forgotten how well you were getting along together at your last meeting. So, as quickly as possible, you should re-establish that rapport using the techniques I have already described.

Agree an agenda

Having established rapport, the next step is to set an agenda for your meeting. Do not be tempted to do this when you first arrange the meeting on the telephone. The sole purpose of your initial contact is to arrange a meeting and agree the time allocated for the meeting. If you attempt to discuss anything else, you could end up with your meeting being cancelled.

You set an agenda by first asking your prospect some questions. The power of this process is that whilst you are asking questions which appear to be giving them control, it is in fact you who are controlling the situation. You could ask questions such as:

'Mrs Smith, what are some of the things you would like to accomplish today?'

or

'What was it about our previous conversation that prompted you to invite me in for this meeting?'

or

'What was it about the information I sent you that made you decide to call me in for this meeting?'

or

'Just so we make the best use of our time today Mrs Smith, can we please quickly put together an agenda of all the points you would like to discuss today and confirm what you'd like to achieve by the end of this meeting?'

Each time they make a point you say: 'Thank you, is there anything in addition to that I should be making a note of?'

When they have finished explaining what they would like to accomplish, you should then bring up the crucial points you would like to add into that agenda. You do this quite subtly by simply saying:

'Thank you, and what about (your crucial point 1)?'

'And what about (your crucial point 2)?'

'And would (your crucial point 3) be important to discuss?'

When you have all the points you want included, you briefly summarise all the agenda items that have been agreed and move on to the next stage in the process.

Get an up-front agreement to your terms

Getting an up-front agreement to doing business your way is an important step in the sales process for a number of reasons:

■ It shows the prospect that you are a professional person and expect to be respected, as they do.

■ It shows the prospect that you value your time and theirs.

■ It is going to eliminate hearing those words that most salespeople dread to hear – 'I want to think it over'.

Here is how you gain that agreement. You say:

John. I'd like to suggest we set some ground rules for this meeting. I assume you are going to want to ask me several questions about my company and our products and services and how we might help you. And I of course would like the opportunity to ask you some questions to make sure I fully understand your business and your concerns. Is that going to be OK with you please?

The only answer they can give you is 'yes'.

Thank you. As we go through that process, you might feel that our product/service is just not right for you. If that happens, rather than us waste each other's time, would you be OK with saying 'no' to me please? You could say something like, 'Let's stop this meeting right now Bruce because I have no interest in this at all.' Are you OK with that?

They have to agree with you. Who could resist the opportunity to say 'no' without hesitation or offence?

Thank you. On the other hand you may feel I have exactly what you need, in which case I'd expect you to say 'yes'. What I hope you won't say is 'I want to think it over'. To be frank, I'd much rather you said 'no'. Are you OK saying 'no' to me John?

Again you have given them the opportunity to say 'no' which they will normally accept. By agreeing to that, they have also, by default, agreed that they will not say 'I want to think it over'!

If this is a simple sale, you can now be reasonably certain you are going to get a 'yes' or a 'no' response to your closing questions. If it is a complex sale, you can expect a 'yes' or 'no' response to moving on to the next stage in the sales process. In most cases, you will not get an 'I want to think it over' response. If you do, you can challenge that politely by saying 'that's not what we agreed'.

Now you may be thinking this is dangerous and you are possibly feeling uncomfortable with this approach. What if they don't agree to buy or move on to the next stage in the sales process? What if they genuinely 'need' to think it over? Here is my view.

Most prospects do not think anything over. They are far too busy; they have 101 other things they have to deal with that are going to prevent them from setting aside time to think it over. Because they haven't done it, they are not going to take your calls, and even if they do – they are likely to say 'no'. Even if they do set aside time to think it over, they are very unlikely to remember precisely what they have to think over and will therefore raise a number of objections in their mind which you will not be there to answer.

> ❝ most prospects do not think anything over ❞

Think back over how many times you had prospects saying 'I want to think it over' and how much time you wasted chasing them afterwards for a decision. You know that most customers or prospects who tell you they are going to 'think it over' very rarely do. I would far sooner not spend my time chasing prospects who said they need to think it over. I would far sooner have a 'yes' and move on to the next stage in the buying process or a 'no' and move on to the next prospect or customer. I advise you to do the same.

I appreciate that my precise choice of words may not always suit your style and you may feel more comfortable amending my suggested script a little. At this point, or as soon as it is convenient to do so, create your own script for establishing an agreement to your terms of business and eliminating 'I want to think it over', and when you are happy with it, transfer it to Exercise 7.1 and learn it off by heart. If you are happy with my version as it is, then learn it off by heart and use that.

exercise 7.1

My script for establishing an agreement to my terms of
business and eliminating 'I want to think it over'

_____

_____

_____

_____

_____

_____

_____

_____

_____

_____

_____

_____

_____

_____

_____

_____

_____

If you prefer not to write in this book, this form and all others are
available to download at www.bruceking.co.uk/doubleyoursales

Establish authority

At some stage in the sales process you may find out that the person you are presenting to is not the person who can make a decision. In a 'worst case scenario', and after making numerous failed attempts to contact your prospect after your initial presentation, you are going to realise that they had no authority to make a decision and, in fact, had been asked by a higher authority to get you to come in for some 'unpaid consulting'. To avoid this, you are going to need to find out if your prospect is the sole decision maker, and if they are not, who else **ff find out if your** will need to be involved in the decision-**prospect is the sole** making process. To save what could be a **decision maker 55** great deal of your precious time, the sooner you find out the better! How do you do this?

I always believe in starting my approach to a prospective client as high up within the organisation as I can. I would far sooner get passed down to somebody with the introduction of the higher authority than get passed up by someone with a lower authority. In taking the 'top down' approach, I have the opportunity to ask that higher authority if they will need to be a part of the decision-making process or if the person they are passing me down to has the authority to make a decision. The other important fact to recognise when approaching people at different levels of authority within an organisation is that a known or unknown problem may be causing a completely different type of pain to different people, but for the same fundamental reason. Here is an example to illustrate this point.

Let us suppose that the XYZ Company has a problem, which is that their sales representatives are spending too much time with customers taking repeat orders that could easily be handled by a small telesales team and, as a result, lack the time to prospect for new customers. As it is a large organisation, not everyone who might want to know or should want to know about this problem may be aware of it. However, the problem still exists and people at different levels within the organisation are going to be experiencing pain as a result, but in a different way. I call this the pain ladder.

■ The CEO may be suffering pain because shareholders are complaining about lower earnings per share and the share price has been falling.

■ The Director of Finance may be suffering pain because of increased operational costs and falling profits.

■ The Director of Sales may be suffering pain because new account revenue generation is not meeting targets.

Each of these categories of people are suffering pain of a different nature, but due to the same problem. So when approaching these people 'top down' you will need to address their specific pain in order to gain their attention.

Taking the example above, you might approach the CEO and suggest you may know one of the reasons their share price is falling and you have a solution to the problem. You would approach the finance director and suggest you may have a solution to the increased operational costs, whilst you would approach the sales director and suggest you have a solution to why salespeople are not able to prospect for new accounts. Same problem – different pains!

If you are unsure if the person you are meeting with is the sole decision maker, then you need to confirm that with them. So you simply ask the question:

> Mrs Smith, in order to ensure I don't take up too much of your time and only give you relevant information, can you please tell me, if you really like what I have to show you, are you the person who will make the decision or does anyone else need to be involved?

If they respond with the fact that they are the only person, you have your decision maker, subject of course to them having told you the truth. If the answer is that others will be involved, here are some of the questions you must ask.

■ *What are their names and titles?* Their titles are particularly important for you to ascertain whether they are above or below the authority level of your prospect.

■ *Will you get the opportunity to present to them as well?* If the answer is 'yes', then you need to confirm what their particular interest will be. If that is on the agreed agenda to discuss, ask your prospect whether it is necessary to discuss it with them or would it be better left to discuss with that other person or people.

If the answer is 'no', you will not get the opportunity to present to the other decision maker(s), but you need to confirm their particular interests are represented on the agenda for you both to discuss. If they are not, get an agreement to add these to the agenda and do so before continuing to the next stage of the sales process.

If the sale is a complex sale and more than one person is going to be involved in the decision-making process, then you also need to establish what the buying process is. By doing so you can make sure you move forward on the appropriate track as quickly as possible. Most prospects will tell you if asked in the correct and non-confrontational way, as early on in your meeting as possible. Say to them:

Janet, assuming you really like what I present to you today, and so that I don't trouble you unnecessarily as we move on, can you please tell me the precise stages in the decision-making process? That way I can make sure I have all the information ready and available for you at the appropriate times.

Once you know the process, you can plan ahead to ensure you move the sale forward in the fastest and most effective way.

Ask 'facts questions'

There are two reasons for asking facts questions and I shall deal with the most important first. I call it 'painting the picture'.

We salespeople often have the audacity, or indeed stupidity, to assume that the moment that we start to speak to prospects, whether on the telephone or face to face, they will automatically forget everything else that is going on in their personal and business lives and put themselves 'in the picture' that we want them to see themselves in. I will illustrate this using an example of how I might approach a prospect to whom I wanted to sell my sales training services.

This is what I know about my prospect from my pre-call research:

■ They are the Sales Director for the inbound telephone marketing division of a large finance corporation.

■ The organisation has 12 offices countrywide.

■ They have 250 staff at each of their offices.

■ They are advertising in national and regional newspapers every week for sales staff.

■ Staff leave or are dismissed frequently.

■ Their profits have fallen by over 15 per cent in the last 12 months compared to the previous year.

■ Their share price has fallen by 6 per cent.

Now that is the picture I want them to be seeing from the moment I walk through their office door so that they can instantly tune in to my thinking and what I am going to present to them. Do you think they will be seeing that picture in their minds the moment I introduce myself? No, they will not! If that is the picture I want them to be seeing, I have to paint it for them. I do not approach this by telling them what I see and what I want them to see, but instead by asking facts questions. I ask questions that I already know the answers to so that they paint the picture for themselves. I will ask:

■ How many offices do you have?

■ How many sales staff do you have at each office?

■ How often do you have to recruit?

■ How often do you lose staff?

■ How much revenue do your average top salespeople – your A grades – bring in?

■ How much revenue do your average B and C grades bring in?

■ What is your budget for training?

I also ask some questions that I do not have the answer to but would like to know. That is the second reason for asking facts questions; to establish facts that I am not aware of but would like to know to complete my picture and theirs.

Note that these are facts questions and are not intended to disturb them. However, as I ask each question and they have to think about their answers, I have them seeing the picture in their minds that I want them to see and I am clarifying my own version of this picture. Now it is time to move on and expose the pain using issue questions.

Ask 'issue questions'

Issue questions are formulated to expose known or unrealised pain and expose opportunities. Following on from the previous example, here are some of the questions I could use to expose the pain and opportunities:

- How difficult is it for you managing 12 offices?
- Is your advertising budget for recruiting a challenge?
- What if you could reduce that budget by at least 50 per cent?
- What issues do you face when staff leave?
- What if you could reduce your staff turnover by 50 per cent or more?
- How do you manage to train staff effectively when they are coming and going on such a regular basis?
- What is the impact of badly trained staff on sales?
- How many customers do you think you lose?
- How much is this problem costing you?
- Who takes a responsibility for a fall in sales?
- How much more time would you have available for training if you weren't so busy interviewing and recruiting?
- How much more profitable would you be if 50 per cent of the Bs and Cs were in your A grade?

Of course I do not ask these questions one after the other. As I ask each one and get a response from my prospect, we will have a discussion on each point before moving on to the next. You can, however, be sure that the prospect is hurting by now because I have exposed a lot of painful areas. I want them hurting a lot more and demonstrating extreme pain. How will you know when a prospect is hurting sufficiently?

Prospects are only hurting sufficiently when they express feelings. Once you have exposed the pain with the above questions, you need to get the prospect to express feelings. To do this, you ask questions such as:

■ How do you feel about that?
■ Do you find this frustrating?
■ How angry does this make you?
■ Do you get very upset about this?
■ How much time do you spend worrying about this?
■ Does your CEO give you a hard time over this?

When your prospect expresses strong feelings, you know they are really hurting. This is the time to present the features and benefits of your product or service – your solution and how it can take their pain away.

The following two exercises (Exercises 7.2 and 7.3 on pages 167 and 168) are headed up *Facts questions* and *Issue questions*. Of course some facts questions and issue questions you ask will vary from prospect to prospect. Some will be the same. List the general facts questions and issue questions you might ask that will be common to most prospects. Some may be the same questions you wrote down in Exercise 3.3. Many should be different because you are no longer selling an appointment; you are now selling your product or service.

Present your features and benefits

Exercise 7.4 that then follows (on page 169) is divided into two columns. On the first of these pages, the columns are headed

Pain/problem exposed and *Features and benefits that solve the problem*. Transfer the *Pain/problems* which you identified in Exercise 2.2 to the first column and then note the features and benefits of your product or service that will solve this pain/problem.

On the second page of Exercise 7.4 (page 170), the columns are headed *Opportunity exposed* and *Features and benefits that will exploit the opportunity*. Transfer the *opportunities exposed* which you identified in Exercise 2.3 to the first column and then note the features and benefits of your product or service that will exploit this opportunity.

exercise 7.2

Facts questions I might ask

_____

_____

_____

_____

_____

_____

_____

_____

_____

_____

_____

_____

_____

_____

_____

_____

_____

_____

_____

If you prefer not to write in this book, this form and all others are available to download at www.bruceking.co.uk/doubleyoursales

exercise 7.3

Issue questions I might ask

exercise 7.4

Pain/problem exposed	Features and benefits that solve the problem

If you prefer not to write in this book, this form and all others are available to download at www.bruceking.co.uk/doubleyoursales

exercise 7.4 (cont.)

Opportunity exposed	Features and benefits that will exploit the opportunity

If you prefer not to write in this book, this form and all others are available to download at www.bruceking.co.uk/doubleyoursales

Case studies

Prospects love to hear stories about what you have been able to achieve for other companies. Stories sell! In our case a story means a case study and in Master Class 3 we discussed using a brief summary of case studies as a way of arousing the prospect's interest in agreeing to meet with us. During the face-to-face presentation we need to have a more detailed case study to demonstrate our skills and effectiveness.

This is the ideal format for presenting a case study:

■ name the client company – of course you will need to obtain their permission to use them as a case study.

■ describe the situation

■ describe the issue

■ describe the reasons for the issue

■ describe your solution

■ give the results.

Here is an example:

---

case study

Company and situation

A situation that illustrates what we have been able to achieve for other companies was with The XYZ Company. They were one of the country's leading suppliers of office stationery products.

The issue

Over a two-year period they lost significant market share to their online competitors and their sales representatives were failing to take on sufficient new accounts to compensate for this. As a result, their profits had fallen by 15 per cent and their share price by 22 per cent, which was causing some consternation amongst the shareholders and the board, as well as affecting the morale of the sales team.

Reasons for the issue

After a detailed analysis of their pricing, sales and marketing process in conjunction with their sales director and the sales team, we determined that the issue was not pricing, but that their sales team were spending too much time taking orders from existing customers. In fact all customers' orders had to be placed through the representative, no matter how small. This left them insufficient time to prospect for and open new accounts.

The solution

We identified several methodologies that would be required to maximise the time a salesperson had to spend generating new business, through prospecting and referral systems, whilst maintaining and increasing purchases from existing customers. We developed a training programme for the sales team, worked with the Finance Director on a new bonus system that encouraged new customer acquisition, and worked on increasing business from existing customers. We also advised on the technological changes that needed to be made to internal systems to facilitate a process whereby customers had a choice of placing orders with the representative or placing orders direct by telephone and online.

The results

The result was that over the following 12 months, the customer base increased by 23 per cent, sales to existing customers increased by 1 per cent, the morale of the sales team was boosted significantly, and the share price rose by 26 per cent.

If you already have some impressive case studies, then ensure you know all the details and can deliver them without reference to notes or printed case studies. If you do not, this is something to brainstorm with your colleagues and make sure you all have some great stories to tell.

The last stages in the ultimate selling system are negotiating, handling objections and closing the sale. In many cases, if you have handled the previous stages in the ultimate selling system well, have established sufficient pain and presented cost effective solutions, then your prospect may be demanding to do business with you.

In other cases you may well have to negotiate, handle objections and close the sale. Each of those activities could take place almost simultaneously. In addition, objections may be raised as a negotiating tactic and negotiations could easily be confused with objections. Sometimes a statement could be either an objection or a negotiating tactic, or indeed both, but for the sake of simplicity I shall deal with each of those subjects and closing the sale as separate activities in the following Master Classes.

Key action points

■ If you do not have a selling system that puts you in control, then you are going to default to the buyer's 'buying system'.

■ The reason for asking facts questions is to get the prospect to see the picture you want them to see and establish facts you were not aware of and need to know.

■ List and learn all the facts questions you can ask to paint your picture.

■ Issue questions are asked to expose known or unrealised pain and known or unrealised opportunities. List and learn all the issue questions you can use to expose pain.

■ Do not present the features and benefits of your product or service until your prospect is expressing strong feelings related to their pain or opportunity.

■ List the features and benefits of your product or service that can solve the prospect's pains and problems and the opportunities you can help them to exploit.

■ Write down and learn the precise words you will use to establish the prospect's authority and the decision-making process.

■ Write down and learn the precise words for getting an up-front agreement to your terms and avoiding 'I want to think it over'.

■ Prepare and/or learn the details of several case studies that demonstrate to a prospect how you have solved various problems or pains for other organisations. Also have these available as printed sales aids.

■ Continue with the *GAVA double your sales – fast* process daily.

■ Please study and work on applying the techniques in this Master Class for at least one week before moving on.

8

Win–win negotiating

The 16 golden rules of successful negotiating

You must never try to make all the money that's in a deal. Let
the other fellow make some money too, because if you have a
reputation for always making all the money, you won't have
many deals.

J. Paul Getty, American industrialist and art collector

The process of negotiation involves a thorough investigation
of what both you and the other person want to achieve and
discovering a mutually acceptable compromise that gives
you both as much of what you want as is achievable.

Negotiation is one of the most difficult aspects of selling and requires
a diverse range of skills, but master negotiation and there is no other
aspect of the sales process that can produce such significant results.

I taught both my daughters the 'flinch technique' from a very
early age. Not only should you be aware of this technique but
you should use it yourself whenever you are buying almost anything. This one technique could save you a small fortune in the
future. It goes like this. You ask the price, even if it is on the label.
Then whatever the response, you visibly flinch and say – 'How
much?!' and sound shocked and horrified.

My daughters have been using the 'flinch technique' from about
the age of eight and almost never fail to get a significant discount,

even in large store chains that supposedly do not give discounts. In my experience – and theirs – everything is negotiable.

The other point I should mention is that negotiation is a way of life in many cultures – and not in others. So if you come from a culture that is not used to negotiating and it makes you feel a little uncomfortable, the thing to do is practise. When you are buying, practise negotiating wherever you are and whatever you are buying. You will soon start to enjoy the experience and want to do more, especially when you see the money it can save you.

You can start small if you prefer. For example, when you next go into a newsagent for a newspaper that normally costs you £1, say to the newsagent, 'Sorry I've only got 90 pence on me. Is that OK?' If they say 'no' – offer to take the one with the slightly creased front page instead. If you still get a 'no', go to another newsagent. I guarantee you will get it for a lower price than a pound. So you saved yourself 10 pence or 10 per cent. Not a lot – but start doing that with items that cost £10 or £100 or £1000 or £10,000 and you are going to be saving yourself a lot of money, and learning while you are doing it. Get used to asking questions like, 'What kind of discount can you offer me today?' and making statements such as, 'I've only got this amount to spend', 'You'll have to do better than that' , 'Wow, that's a lot more than I wanted to pay', and flinch when you make them!

Who has the power in negotiations?

Before I move on to some specific negotiation rules and tech-niques, let's first take a look at who has the power or upper hand when negotiating? When I ask this question in a Master Class, almost without exception, people say the buyer has all the power. That is simply not true. The person who has the power is the person who thinks they have the power and just because you are the seller does not mean you do not. The buyer is not usually going to waste their time negotiating with you if they do not have any interest in your product or service; and you do not have to sell to them if you choose not to. They cannot possibly be the only customer left on the planet. So, who has the power? It is the person who thinks they have! And when you think you have the power, your whole attitude to the negotiation process changes to your advantage.

Neither should you be intimidated by your buyer's status. People in high positions, who may have a string of qualifications and letters after their name and sit on the board of directors, are not necessarily smarter than you. Learn the selling skills in these Master Classes and all there is to know about your product or service and you can hold the power with confidence, no matter how smart your prospect appears to be.

It is also rare for anyone to have a totally unique product or service that nobody else offers and which the buyer desperately wants. If that were the case, there is no question where the power would lie; but even in those circumstances the astute buyer will still want to negotiate. Most times, however, you do have competition and the buyer will make it clear to you that they can go elsewhere if you cannot meet their terms. You must therefore do whatever you can to create the impression that your product or service is unique. How do you do that when it is not? It is very simple when you realise that there is more to your package than just what your company has to offer. It is also about you and you are the one factor that is absolutely unique. You can therefore create a unique offering by virtue of the way you conduct yourself, how you build rapport, empathy and trust with your prospect and how you can add value to the product or service on a long-term basis when you become a trusted adviser.

That also means that negotiation should never become aggressive or confrontational. The only time that might work is if it is a one-off sale and you are never likely to want to sell to this person ever again. A classic example of that situation could be when you are buying or selling your own home. You are never likely to be buying or selling another of your homes to that same person, so you do not have to consider any ongoing relationship and the effect your negotiations might have on them and any future negotiation. That is one of the reasons why buying a home is frequently one of the most stressful situations in life. So if you are not selling your home, or carpets or souvenirs to a tourist in a marketplace at grossly inflated prices, it's probably best to forget that style of negotiation and talk about negotiation that works for both parties; in other words win–win, or collaborative negotiation. That is where everyone thinks they have walked away a winner and feels happy with the result.

Prepare, prepare, prepare

You would not go deep sea diving without considerable preparation. Neither should you negotiate without prior preparation. You can rest assured that if you are dealing with a professional buyer, they will be well prepared. As I mentioned in an earlier Master Class, professional buyers often have more training in buying and negotiating than most salespeople have in selling. If you are not prepared, they are definitely going to have the upper hand. Even if you are not dealing with a trained negotiator, they will still want the best possible price and the highest quality of product or service for that price; so preparation is essential and the higher the value and complexity of your product or service, the more preparation you should undertake.

One of the best negotiators I have ever met was a Chinese gentleman called Lim Tzun. Lim was remarkable in many ways but particularly because of his ability to make even the most complex of situations appear simple. When it came to negotiation, he used what he called 'LIM's strategy for preparing to negotiate', which are a set of rules:

- The 'L' In LIM's rules stands for Love to have. Define the very best possible outcome you could wish for.
- The 'I' in LIM's rules stands for Intention. Define your most realistic, high-level outcome.
- The 'M' in LIM's rules stands for Must have. This is the least you are prepared to accept or you will walk away.

Use LIM's strategy as the starting point for preparing for any negotiation and, along with the other techniques you will learn in this Master Class, you will always come out of your negotiations with a satisfactory result and not fall into the trap of giving away too much and regretting it afterwards. You should also think about what your buyer's aspirations might be and you can use LIM's strategy for that process too.

Know your negotiation variables

As part of your preparation, you must also know all of the variables you can negotiate on if you have to.

In most negotiations you are going to have to make some concessions. Whether or not you can negotiate on price, there should be countless other factors that can form part of your negotiations. These could include:

■ getting all of the project rather than the part of the project
■ delivery times or delivery methods
■ changing the size of the order
■ changing the specification
■ offering a different model
■ getting advance payments or deferring payments
■ standard colours rather than custom colours
■ ownership of the tooling
■ limited or extended guarantees
■ installation charges
■ training requirements
■ lower or variable servicing costs.

This list could be considerably longer and will depend a great deal on what you are selling. So rather than making any more suggestions myself, now or as soon as is convenient, in Exercise 8.1 (overleaf), make a complete list of every single aspect of your product or service offering that could be negotiated. No matter how trivial it might seem to you, add it to the list.

The items you list are your variables, bargaining chips and possible concessions; the more, the better. Allocate them real financial value during your preparation for negotiation and you are far less likely to have to reduce your price when you bargain with these.

exercise 8.1

List everything about your product, service or package that could be negotiable:

_____

_____

_____

_____

_____

_____

_____

_____

_____

_____

_____

_____

_____

_____

_____

_____

_____

_____

If you prefer not to write in this book, this form and all others are available to download at www.bruceking.co.uk/doubleyoursales

Decide on level of authority

As part of your preparation you must also decide the level of authority you want your prospect to believe you have.

This is a topic which I find many of the very best negotiators have neglected to take into account when deciding on their negotiating strategy; yet it can be a very powerful tool in the negotiation process. A negotiator with limited authority becomes much harder to negotiate with – and when the other person wants a fast result and the sticking point is something beyond their level of authority, they have to find a way around that point, or risk delaying or forgoing their purchase.

As a seller, even if you are the CEO or MD, or the owner/manager, and the buyer knows you are, you can still refer to a higher authority. That authority could be your investors, your bank manager, your accountant, your lawyer, your suppliers, or indeed anyone else who might be involved in financing or delivering the product or service. Therefore, before going into a negotiation, irrespective of your position and title, decide what limits you want to impose on your level of authority.

Rehearse

Finally, on preparation: rehearse, rehearse, rehearse.

If you have ever carried out role playing with other members of your team, particularly the sales team, you will know that when you are the seller and they are acting the buyer, they almost always turn out to be the nightmare customer you hope never to meet. I believe it is their way of getting back at someone for all the tough selling situations they have faced in the past.

These are the very people you need to rehearse your presentation and negotiations with. They will almost certainly give you the most difficult time, and will also want to help you overcome just about anything a tough negotiator is going to put you through.

16 golden rules for successful negotiating

1 Remember who you work for

It should always be your intention to develop great relationships with customers and earn their trust and respect in order to become a trusted adviser. Nevertheless, just as it is the buyer's responsibility to get the best possible deal for their company, your responsibility is to secure the best possible deal for you and your company – not the customer. Just because you do that does not mean you lose the respect and trust of the customer. It is just as easy to maintain that trust and respect and still be firm when negotiating. Remember you also have a responsibility to your other customers. You can easily ruin a relationship with an existing customer by offering a new customer better terms.

2 Do not trust your assumptions

Almost all negotiation starts with assumptions being made on both sides. For example, you may be thinking:

- They'll never pay that much, or
- They need it too quickly, or
- There's lots of other companies competing for this business, or
- They wouldn't like our other options, or
- We're not going to be able to make the best offer.

Making assumptions like this can destroy you before you have even started. They lower your expectations, influence the outcome of the negotiation and, in many cases, are simply incorrect. It is perfectly all right to make assumptions – you have to start somewhere – you just must not believe them. The purpose of negotiation is to check those assumptions out and see if they are right or wrong.

3 Aim high

Your starting price and terms for your negotiations should be the highest you could possibly justify for your product or service.

The closer your starting point is to what you are prepared to accept, the less you have left to negotiate with and the less likely you are to be happy with the outcome.

A classic, although not necessarily sophisticated, negotiating tactic which will often be used on you by your prospect is the 'split the difference' technique. You state your price, the buyer makes a deliberately very low offer, and after a little discussion they raise their offer a tiny bit and then suggest you split the difference. If you started low, you do not come out of it too well if you agree to the split. Remember that it is very easy to get drawn into agreeing to this offer because it sounds fair. Most times it is not and does not create a win–win situation. The buyer knows it is not fair and you can always say 'no'.

4 Never start negotiating until there is some commitment in principle to do business

If you negotiate without the prospect having given a firm indication that they are seriously considering doing business with you, you leave yourself in a weaker position where you will almost certainly have to negotiate even better terms further down the line. So if you do not have that commitment in principle, do not negotiate. If you do not have that commitment or are unsure, ask a question like: 'If we can agree the details, when will you be going ahead?' or 'What else do we need to discuss before we get into the details, so we both know there's an intention of moving this forward and placing an order?', followed, of course, by the silent close. Until you have a positive response – there is nothing to negotiate.

5 Avoid making the first offer

It is a fact that whoever makes the first offer is at a disadvantage, so wherever possible – do not. You would be amazed how often a buyer will offer a price or state a budget they have available that is way above what you were anticipating, and that gives you an opportunity to reframe your entire proposal to take into account that higher than expected price or budget. It is equally amazing how often they do not offer that higher price because they insisted on hearing the seller's offer first, and the seller did not start high enough.

By contrast, sometimes the buyer will make a ridiculously low offer. If they do, you can simply refuse to negotiate at all. They knew it was a silly offer when they made it, and by refusing to negotiate you put them in a position where they have to come back with a better one.

6 Never accept the first offer

You should never accept the first offer, no matter how good it is, for two reasons. Firstly, the other party is very likely to hand you some additional concessions if asked, and secondly, if you do, they may well think the offer they made was too good or foolish and will want to go back on it later. You make a big mistake if you take the first offer. Instead – flinch and say something like 'is that the best you can do?' or 'is there anything else you could do for me that would make that work well for both of us'; followed, of course, by the 'silent close'.

❝ you make a big mistake if you take the first offer ❞

7 Never give away concessions

Concessions are for trading, not giving away; so never give anything away without getting something in return. If you do, you are not negotiating at all, you are giving in.

There is also another excellent reason for not giving away concessions. A concession given away too easily does not make the person who won it feel good, because they got it far too easily. You must therefore always ask for something in return. It could be as simple as 'If I do that for you, will you sign an order today?'

8 'Put yourself in my shoes – put yourself in their shoes'

Empathy is the process of identifying with another person's situation and emotions. Creating empathy is another, often underused, negotiating tactic.

When I am in a difficult negotiating situation, I like to get the other party to see themselves in my position. That way they get more involved and get a better idea of my concerns and possible limitations. This moves us both to look for a real win–win solution. So when things are getting a little difficult, just say – 'put yourself in my shoes' – and see how well most people react.

By the same token, you should put yourself in other people's shoes and use empathy. For example, when someone says to you that they think your price is too high and they are looking upset, but you are really not able to reduce the price, you could say:

> I think you are upset that I'm not able to reduce the price and I can understand why. Please be assured I am committed to working with you and making this deal work for both of us. Let's see what else we can do to help each other come to a satisfactory solution.

9 Say 'no' when you mean 'no'

I have noticed so many times in negotiations that people say a variety of things when they really mean 'no'; but because they are scared of the response to a 'no', they say something else instead. They will make statements such as:

- 'It might be possible.'
- 'Let me think on that.'
- 'Maybe.'
- 'I'll see what I can do.'
- 'I'll let you know on that point.'

The problem with making these statements when you really mean 'no' is that it creates an unnecessary delay in the negotiation process, and an expectation in the buyer's mind which cannot be fulfilled. If what they are asking for is not possible for any reason, the time to say 'no' is right then. An honest 'No, that's just not possible', with an appropriate explanation delivered with empathy for the buyer's situation, is all that is necessary and demonstrates your professionalism, empathy and authority.

10 Use only two or three strong points at most for not agreeing to a concession

There is often a temptation to give as many reasons as possible as to why you cannot agree to a concession that is being demanded of you. That is usually a mistake because two or three at most will be really strong reasons for you to decline. The rest will have been included in the hope of strengthening your argument.

A good negotiator will ignore your strong reasons and go straight to your weakest points. When they destroy those reasons, they will put you in a position where it is difficult to go back and start talking about the stronger ones. Keep to the two or three most powerful reasons why you cannot comply with a request for a concession and be sure you can support those reasons.

11 Give yourself sufficient time to negotiate

If it is going to need hours, weeks or months to negotiate properly, than make sure you have the hours, weeks or months. The person who is under time pressure is always at a disadvantage and you can use this to your advantage when negotiating. You can speed the process up or slow it down and, by doing so, put subtle pressure on the other party to agree to your proposals and conditions.

Along with time goes patience. It takes time to fully understand all the issues, weigh up the risks and understand the other party's expectations. It also takes patience to let the other party get used to the fact that what they might want may not be possible and they have to settle for less. Quick negotiations do not give time for this and can work against you.

12 Keep notes

Keep detailed notes of everything that has been agreed and clarify them as you go. Make sure your buyer sees you are taking those notes and ensure they confirm their agreement to every point of the negotiation. If you do not you will often find the buyer conveniently forgets some of the things they agreed to that were not in their favour. If the meeting is one of a series, also ensure you confirm those agreements in writing before the next meeting.

❝ confirm agreements in writing ❞

13 Keep the BIG picture in mind at all times

Another technique used by well trained negotiators is what I call the 'orange technique'. The way most people eat an orange is to first peel it and then either remove and eat one segment at a time or divide the entire orange into segments, and then eat them one at a time.

What the well trained negotiator may want to do with you is to try to distract you from looking at your big picture by going over one segment of your proposal at a time and attempting to gain as large a concession as possible from you on that point before discussing any other aspect of your proposals. If you get drawn into this, you may find that the series of concessions you gave over numerous aspects of your proposals, which may have seemed reasonable at the time you conceded each one, add up to massively more than you would ever have agreed to if you kept the big picture in mind.

14 Watch out for 'nibblers'

Nibbling is one of the negotiating techniques I use frequently and with great success when I am buying something of some significant value. Here is one example of how I have used 'nibbling' in the past to secure some significant savings, to illustrate how the technique works.

A few years ago, I was considering investing in a holiday home in Portugal. It was a modest villa being built on a private estate overlooking the sea. A luxury gym and health spa was also being built on the site which, according to the developer's literature, residents could have access to for 50 per cent of the normal substantial annual membership fee. I deliberately chose not to mention this in any of our conversations and negotiations.

After several meetings with the developers negotiating the price, the quality and design of the various fixtures and fittings that were to be included, and numerous other points, I was finally ready to sign the contract. So there we were, my wife and I, sitting in the developer's office. You could see the look of relief on the faces of the Sales Director and his second in command now that the negotiations had finally come to an end. What they did not know was that I had one final, large nibble to come.

The sales director placed the contracts neatly on the table, whilst his second in command was pouring out four glasses of cold white wine to toast the deal. I sat down in front of the paperwork, picked up the pen and held it close to the point where I was to sign. I paused, looked up and said 'This does include free lifetime membership of the gym and health spa doesn't it?' (silent close).

There was a lengthy silence and you could see by the non-verbal exchanges taking place that the last thing they wanted to do was to start negotiating with me all over again. After a short while, the Sales Director said, 'Mr King, it does not, but providing you promise not to mention it to any other investor, we'd be happy to include that, just for you and your wife.'

'Thank you,' I said. 'If you'd just write that in on the contract just here and initial it, I can sign and we can all sit down and enjoy that glass of wine.' That nibble saved me £4000 a year and so far we've enjoyed that free membership for seven years!

> **££ nibbling is likely to be used on you frequently ¥¥**

Nibbling is likely to be used on you frequently, and by knowing it can happen, you are at least prepared. If the nibble is not acceptable to you, don't agree to it. I would certainly have gone ahead with the purchase of that villa, irrespective of whether I got the free lifetime membership or not, as I would have gone ahead with hundreds of other major and minor purchases in the past if my nibble had been turned down.

15 Dealing with 'take it or leave it'

When a prospect tells you to 'take it or leave it', they may genuinely have come to a point where they are not prepared to negotiate any further or they may still be prepared to negotiate. The biggest mistake you could make if the proposed deal was worse than your 'walk away' position would be to walk away from the negotiation. Here are some other questions you could ask to test the prospect's position and continue the negotiation before you do decide to walk away:

- 'If you were in my shoes, how would you react to the pressure of being told to take it or leave it?'
- 'Why, in your opinion should I take it?'
- 'Why is there a pressure to bring these negotiations to a close?'
- 'Are there any other suggestions you could make that we haven't covered yet that might enable me to take it?'
- 'On a scale of nought to 10, if nought means there's no way we could ever agree a deal and 10 means you are ready to go ahead, where are you on that scale?'

When you get a response, you say

- 'What else could I do to get you from there to a 10?'
- 'Could you suggest anything else that might help us to close the gap between where you are and where I am please?'

And finally, number 16

Never accept a final 'no' from anyone who does not have the authority to say 'yes'!

If your proposals are rejected by someone who does not have the authority to go ahead, and you have attempted to negotiate an agreement that was fair to both parties, if all else fails – go to the higher authority and start again. Most times, you have nothing to lose and everything to gain.

Becoming a great negotiator takes time, discipline and practice. Learn all these negotiation tactics and techniques and put them into practice consistently.

Key action points

■ Practise negotiating whenever you are buying anything.

■ The person who has the power in a negotiation is the person who thinks they have.

■ Prepare thoroughly for all negotiations and rehearse.

■ Know all your variables or bargaining chips and assign a financial value to them on a case-by-case basis. Complete the exercise and list all the variables associated with your product or service.

■ Learn and implement the 16 golden rules for successful negotiation.

■ Continue with the *GAVA double your sales – fast* process daily.

■ Please study and work on applying the techniques in this Master Class for at least one week before moving on.

9

Handling objections

Turning objections into opportunities

So many objections may be made to everything, that nothing
can overcome them but the necessity of doing something.
Samuel Johnson, author and lexicographer

xamine the quotation above and you quickly see how it
relates to the importance of exposing pain. The more pain
you can expose and the more it hurts, the less likely a
prospect is to raise objections. However, human nature being
what it is, you must expect to get some objections from time to
time and need to be prepared to deal with them.

I have heard some sales trainers describe an objection as merely
a request for further information. Frankly, I think this is non-
sense. The dictionary definition of objection is 'an expression,
statement or feeling of opposition or dislike'. My thesaurus lists
the following words as suitable alternatives: *censure, counter-argu-
ment, doubt, exception, niggle, protest* and *opposition*. How,
therefore, could anyone describe an objection as simply a request
for further information? That type of attitude to what is often a
genuine initial rejection of your proposals, or part of your proposal, could easily lead to your failure to secure an order.

The three types of objections

There are three basic types of objections that prospects may raise. These are imagined objections, pretend objections and valid objections. Let us take a closer look at these.

Imagined objections

The imagined objection is just that – a figment of your prospect's imagination. The following are typical examples of imagined objections:

- We couldn't afford it.
- I couldn't afford the running costs of this car; it's probably too heavy on fuel.
- I don't know if my wife would like it.
- I don't think it would fit.
- I don't think this carpet will match my curtains.
- I don't think I could get the board to agree.

Now look at these statements again with my comments in brackets. It will then be obvious that these could all be imagined objections.

- We couldn't afford it.

  [Your prospect does not know the cost or what credit or other terms are available.]
- I couldn't afford the running costs of this car; it's probably too heavy on fuel.

  [They do not yet know that although the engine is larger, the new, improved fuel injection system increases fuel economy by 25 per cent.]
- I don't know if my wife would like it.

  [He hasn't asked her yet.]
- I don't think it would fit.

  [She hasn't measured it yet.]
- I don't think this carpet will match my curtains.

[He has not yet seen them together.]

■ I don't think I could get the board of directors to agree.

[He has not asked them yet.]

Pretend objections

What about pretend objections? Probably the most frequent pretend objection you get is when a prospect claims to be too busy to see you. How many times has that been said to you? It is obviously a pretend objection. If I were to telephone you and told you that you had just won the Lottery, that I had a cheque for you for £5 million pounds and just needed 15 minutes with you to complete the paperwork and give you the money, would you find the time in your very busy schedule to see me?

Other frequent pretend objections include:

■ We cannot afford it.

■ It's not in the budget.

■ I don't have the authority to make the decision.

■ We just bought one.

■ We have a contract with our current suppliers.

■ I have to discuss it with...

Valid objections

Valid objections are just what the title suggests. They are legitimate and real reasons why people may not be able to purchase your product or service from you and therefore are likely to be the most difficult to deal with. Nevertheless, you can still deal with them on most occasions.

Having spent many years teaching thousands of people to sell a huge variety of products and services, it has become apparent to me it is very rare indeed that more than six valid objections can be made against any particular aspect of any product or service.

It is essential to know all the imagined, pretend and valid objections that can be levelled against what you are selling, and to rehearse responses to them. What I often find is that what one person in a company's sales force is finding difficulty dealing with, another finds very easy – so again, this is an exercise you could brainstorm with your colleagues.

Carry out Exercise 9.1 now, or as soon as it is convenient, and complete the first column in the objections type table. Make a list of every single objection you can think of that has been raised against your product or service in the first column. In the next column, put an I for imagined, P for pretend or V for valid against it. In some cases you may want to put two or even all three.

exercise 9.1

Objections type table

Objection	I – P – V

If you prefer not to write in this book, this form and all others are available to download at www.bruceking.co.uk/doubleyoursales

The basic rules for handling objections

1 Respect imagined and pretend objections

Earlier in the book we discussed the fact that people like to do business with people they like. Among the several attributes you must develop to become a top salesperson is the ability to make someone like you, want to do business with you and come to rely on you as a trusted adviser. Therefore, the most fundamental principle you must come to terms with when dealing with objections of any kind, is never to argue and never to let the experience of handling an objection develop into a confrontation. Whilst you may know that an objection is either imagined or pretend, you must always treat it as if it were valid. Nobody likes to be ignored or treated as if they were foolish, and dealing with every type of objection as if it were a valid one will gain you the respect and trust of your prospect.

2 Acknowledge the objection before responding

Whenever you are responding to an objection, always start by acknowledging it. It tells the prospect you have heard and accept what they have said. For example, when the prospect says to you, 'It's more than we wanted to pay Bruce', you start your response with 'I appreciate it's more than you wanted to pay Phil, and ... (your response).'

Not only does this tell their conscious mind that you are listening, but because you are mirroring their speech, it is also telling their subconscious mind that you are just like them, they like you, can trust you and would like to do business with you.

3 Listen and let them finish

When I am presenting at a conference or workshop, I ask the attendees to raise their hands if they like to be interrupted when they are speaking. Not a single hand ever goes up. Then I ask how many of them interrupt other people when they are speaking. A sea of hands arise. Do you interrupt prospects when they are raising an objection or asking a question and taking rather a long time in doing so? I'll guess you do.

Why would you do this? You invest time in finding the prospect, researching their background, making the initial contact and securing an appointment. You invest time establishing rapport, asking facts questions, issue questions, and then presenting how your product or service can help them solve their problems and exploit opportunities. You invest a lot of time and effort in your prospect. So why, when they raise an objection or ask a question, do you interrupt them and risk ruining the relationship and losing the sale when you were so close to getting the result you wanted. Nobody wants to do business with people who interrupt them.

From now on, no matter how many times you have heard the question or objection before, listen and let them finish. No matter how bored you are of hearing the same old thing, time after time, which you could immediately respond to, you must look interested, nod, smile and let them know you are taking them seriously. Then use the 'pause, think, respond' technique.

The 'pause, think, respond' technique

Even if you know the answer to it because you have heard the question many times before, do not immediately blurt it out. *Pause* and look as if you are taking the question very seriously and are *thinking* about it. Whether it is an imagined, pretend or valid objection, your prospect needs to know you are taking it seriously. Then you can *respond*.

4 Ask them to elaborate

Sometimes prospects will have a genuine objection, but because they feel under pressure or are just not good at phrasing what they are thinking in a clear and concise manner, what they say is not necessarily what they mean. Ask them to elaborate, posing questions such as 'I don't understand, can you explain that to me?' or 'What do you mean exactly?' followed by the silent close.

Asking them to elaborate, rather than coming back with an immediate response, achieves a number of things.

- It gives them a little more time and takes the pressure off them.
- It will give you a clearer understanding of their concern.
- It makes them feel in control.
- It makes them feel they are maybe a little smarter than you.

That last point is particularly important. Whilst prospects want to deal with intelligent and professional people who are going to provide the highest quality of service to them, they can also be a little wary of people they think may be much smarter than they are, particularly salespeople. Asking them to elaborate and even playing a little dumb from time to time often makes them feel a lot more comfortable with you and they are therefore more likely to open up and tell you what is really concerning them. One of my mentors calls this 'the Colombo' technique after the famous TV detective. Here are some examples of how asking questions in response to some typical objections can be so effective.

'I'm happy with our current supplier'

Your question: 'I appreciate you're happy with your current suppliers. Does that also mean you will never look at other potential suppliers and alternatives in the market?' *or*

'What would have to happen for you to take a fresh look at the competition?' *or*

'Is there one thing about their product or service you'd like to see improved?'

Another way your prospect may put that might be:

'I don't think you could do better than our current supplier?'

To which your response could be: 'What would "better" look like to you?'

'I don't have time to see you.'

Your question: 'What would you need to know from me that would make you want to set aside 20 to 25 minutes to see me?'

'I'd have a problem signing the order today.'

You could respond: 'May I ask you a question – why would that be a problem?'

The other advantage of asking a prospect to elaborate on an objection is that, in many cases, they will talk themselves out of it without you having to say anything. This is particularly true of imagined or pretend objections. Many times I have asked a prospect to elaborate and, after a lengthy silence and possibly some waffled explanation, they have agreed, without any prompting from me, that the objection was in fact irrelevant.

5 Identify all the real objections

When a prospect feels under pressure or a little unsure, they will often stall the process by blurting out the first thing that comes to mind. If you respond promptly and satisfactorily to the first, they will just raise another. Therefore the technique you should use is to get all of the objections out in the open before responding to any of them. Very often it is only the last one that is, in fact, a genuine objection.

When the first objection is raised, you say: 'Just supposing we could get around that' or, 'Just supposing that wasn't an issue, is there anything else that is stopping you from going ahead?' (silent close).

If they raise another objection, you repeat that same question and keep doing that until all their objections are out in the open and they say, 'No – nothing else.'

Then you ask, 'So if I can satisfy you totally on each of those points, will you be going ahead?' (silent close). If the response to that is 'No', you still have not got all of the objections out in the open and need to ask again, 'What else would be stopping you going ahead then?' If the answer is 'Yes', only then do you answer the objections.

6 Confirm they are no longer an objection

Once you have answered an objection it is absolutely essential that you get your prospect's agreement that it no longer exists. Do not assume that because you have answered it to your satisfaction you have answered it to theirs. Ask, 'Have I covered that to your satisfaction?' (silent close), or 'Are you now satisfied completely on that point?' (silent close), or 'Is there anything else you need to know on that subject before I continue?' (silent close). Getting your prospect's confirmation that the objection no longer exists removes the likelihood of them raising it again later. An objection that has not been satisfactorily answered and confirmed as no longer relevant by your prospect, can always be brought up again.

Another useful technique you can use during this process, and one which is particularly effective when dealing with visually dominant prospects, is to write down in a list each of the objections raised. Write clearly and neatly and in full view of your prospect. As you deal with each objection and get their confirmation that it is no longer an issue, you draw a line through that objection. When you have got to the end of the list and every objection has a line through it, it is a very clear visual illustration to the prospect and a confirmation to their subconscious mind that they have no choice now but to keep their agreement to go ahead.

7 Replace 'but' and 'however' with 'and'

Having listened to thousands of salespeople answering objections, I know that you too often use the words 'but' and 'however' when responding to objections. For example, your prospect says to you, 'It's more than we wanted to pay John' and you respond, 'I appreciate it's more than you wanted to pay Phil *but* (or *however*) let me run through the figures again and show you why it's going to give you such an excellent return on your investment.'

Make no mistake about this, the words 'but' and 'however' are argumentative. They are a direct assault on the prospect's conscious and subconscious mind. You are effectively telling the prospect that they are wrong and you are right. On a conscious and subconscious level, you are raising a potentially insurmountable barrier between you and your prospect. You have possibly lost more business through using these words than anything else you could have done or said. In future, replace the words 'but' and 'however' with *and*. Always remember that 'but' and 'however' separate people: '*and*' joins people together.

For example:

> 'It's more than we wanted to pay Bruce.'
>
> 'I appreciate it's more than you wanted to pay Phil AND let me run through the figures again and show you why it's going to give you such an excellent return on your investment.'

Do you see how much more effective this is going to be?

8 The 'feel, felt, found' technique

The feel, felt, found technique works so well with every prospect, and particularly when used with kinaesthetics. This is an example of what you would say, tailored of course to your specific product or service.

> I understand exactly how you FEEL June. Many of our clients FELT exactly the same way when we first presented this solution to them. What they FOUND was that their (return on investment) was far better than they had expected and they have all become long-term clients of ours.

Now look at the structure of that paragraph:

- *'I understand exactly how you FEEL.'* This demonstrates that you empathise with their concern, that you understand them and are on their side.
- *'Many of our clients FELT exactly the same way. . . .'* This demonstrates that it is quite all right for them to feel that way and that there is nothing unusual about how they feel.
- *'What they FOUND was. . . .'* This demonstrates the benefits your other clients received as a result of their purchase.

Price objections

If there is one thing for certain that most prospects will want to negotiate on, it is price, and price objections can be presented to you in a number of ways. A common statement voiced by a prospect will be 'It's too expensive.' Note I used the word 'statement'. They did not ask a question such as 'How much can you reduce it by?', they just made a statement. Therefore even if you have the authority to reduce your price, this is not the time to start doing so.

The statement 'It's too expensive', should be responded to with a question from you, either 'Which means?' (silent close) or 'So where do we go from here?' (silent close). In using either of these responses, you are passing the decision on what to do back to your prospect, which serves two purposes. Firstly, it makes them think they are in control because you have given them a choice and, secondly, and more importantly, it means they have to make the next move.

I used this technique with a prospect just a few weeks ago when I quoted them my highest rate for a five-day conference tour in India and they responded with 'It's too expensive'. When I asked 'So where do we go from here Ramin?' (silent close), I was met with a slight pause, followed by the response, 'I suppose we'll have to increase the ticket price a little then.' Whenever you are faced with a price objection, do not automatically start thinking of reducing your price. There may be many other ways the prospect can meet your quoted price.

The prospect may come back with the same price objection, perhaps worded slightly differently, such as in, 'It's definitely more than we want to spend.' You could respond to this second price objection with the question: 'That's not unusual. Off the record, in round numbers, what price were you hoping for?' (silent close).

Of course it is not 'off the record', but a prospect's subconscious mind hears those words and associates them with genuinely being 'off the record'. This, combined with the words 'round numbers', puts the prospect off guard and makes them much more likely to tell you what they were actually hoping to pay, and are prepared to pay, than giving you a price way below as would often happen in a price negotiation. Another way of identifying what their price point is could be to ask the question: 'In round numbers, off the record, how much too much is it?' (silent close).

Now let us take a specific example to illustrate how to deal with the response you may get from that last question. Let us suppose you are selling a piece of machinery at a cost of £150,000 and they have raised their second price objection. In response to your question, 'In round numbers Peter, off the record, how much too much is it?', they say '£15,000'. Now you have two choices. You can either reduce the price or you can...

Focus on the price difference

I never want to reduce my prices without getting an equivalent financial benefit by restructuring the deal. However, in this case, let us say that there is no margin to reduce the price and no restructuring possible. By focusing on the price difference of £15,000 you now have the prospect fixed on a much smaller sum of money than the total price you were first discussing. Here is how your presentation and response to this price objection should go now. You will probably need a calculator to hand so you can work out the precise figures easily as you work through the process.

You: Let's look at the numbers Peter. This machine is going to last at least five years before it needs replacing. Agreed?

Prospect: Yes.

You: And you said you are open six days a week, 49 weeks a year, yes?

Prospect: Yes.

You: And the factory is operating two, seven-hour a day shifts. That was correct wasn't it?

Prospect: Yes.

You: So this machine is going to be running and saving you money for at least 14 hours a day, six days a week, 49 weeks a year, for at least five years, which is 20,580 hours. And you said it's £15,000 too expensive. That works out at 73p an hour. Is 73p an hour really going to be an issue? (silent close).

If what you are proposing to your client is going to make financial sense, work out the figures on the above basis as they apply to your product or service, and take this approach of focusing on the price difference before ever thinking about restructuring the deal or reducing the price.

Dealing with – 'I have to discuss it with...'

Sometimes you may forget to establish early on in your presentation that the person you are speaking to has the authority to purchase. Other times, in spite of the fact that they had told you they do have the authority, they will still use the classic stall – 'I have to discuss it with.... .' Now here is the challenge; they are either telling the truth or they are not, and you do not know which is correct.

If they had told you earlier that they had the authority to purchase then your response to this stall should simply be, 'That is not what you told me earlier. Why have you changed your mind?' (silent close). Yes, it may appear confrontational, but said quietly and pleasantly it does not need to sound that way. They either told you a lie or they have changed the terms you agreed to, so you are perfectly entitled to ask that question and expect an answer.

If they had not told you that they had the authority because you forgot to ask, or they are adamant that in spite of the fact they had, they still have to discuss it with someone else, you then ask this key question:

> Would you like to go ahead and will you be recommending this?

If they seem unsure or say 'No', then you have not sold them on your product or service. They still have concerns that need addressing and it is now up to you to start questioning again to identify the reasons why. When you have done that satisfactorily, you may well find that they no longer have to discuss it with anyone and that they were simply using that as an excuse because they were not convinced. If you had not asked that question, it is almost certain you would have lost the sale.

If, on the other hand, they say 'Yes', then you need to ask a number of other questions. These could include:

- 'Would you like me to present our proposals with you?' This is, of course, the best option for you.
- 'What help, information or other materials do you need from me in order to present this to them so they do agree?'

If they genuinely want to recommend they go ahead, you need to ensure as far as possible that they present your proposal in the best way available and have all the supporting materials required to do so.

Dealing with – 'I want to think about it'

In a previous Master Class I showed you how to establish the 'up-front agreement', to avoid the prospect saying they want to think it over. Sometimes you will forget to set up the agreement and other times, in spite of the fact that they agreed, they may change their minds. If they have agreed not to think it over and still raise that objection, your response should be to say, 'That is not what we agreed' (silent close).

If you omitted to get an up-front agreement, or they still insist on thinking it over, then this is the process you go through.

You: I appreciate you may want to think about it. Generally speaking, when a client says something like that to me, it means I haven't explained something properly. So please tell me – what is it I've not made clear – is it the (name any one feature of your product or service that you think may have caused the objection e.g. cost/size/service intervals)?

Prospect: It's the cost of it.

You: I can understand that cost may be an issue. In addition to that, is there anything else that's stopping you from going ahead? (silent close).

Prospect: No.

You: So if we can deal satisfactorily with the investment required, is there any reason why we couldn't go ahead today? (silent close).

Prospect: No.

As I stated at the beginning of this chapter, the more pain you can expose and the more it hurts, the less likely a prospect is to raise objections. Nevertheless, objections will come up from time to time and the more effectively you can handle them using these techniques, the easier it will become to double your sales.

The final exercise in this Master Class is to transfer all the objections you have previously had some difficulty responding to from the objections type table (Exercise 9.1) to the table in Exercise 9.2. Then, on the basis of what you have learned in this Master Class, note how you might respond to them in the future with a question or statement.

exercise 9.2

Objections and responses table

Objection	Response

If you prefer not to write in this book, this form and all others are available to download at www.bruceking.co.uk/doubleyoursales

Key action points

■ Brainstorm with your colleagues all the imagined, pretend and valid objections that can be raised to your product or service and enter these on the objections type table with the appropriate annotation.

■ Learn and put into practice all the basic rules for handling objections.

■ Learn and put into practice the way to deal with price objections.

■ Learn and put into practice the process for dealing with 'I have to discuss it with....'

■ Learn and put into practice the process for dealing with 'I want to think about it.'

■ Transfer all the objections you have previously had some difficulty responding to from the objections type table to the objections and responses table and note how you might respond to them in the future with a question or statement.

■ Continue with the *GAVA double your sales – fast* process daily.

■ Please study and work on applying the techniques in this Master Class for at least one week before moving on.

10

Closing the sale
The 10 best closes

Always be closing. That doesn't mean you are always closing
the deal, but it does mean that you are always closing on the
next step in the process.

Shane Gibson, sales and leadership coach

I hear a lot of sales trainers and salespeople complain about the
use of the term 'closing a sale'. One of the criticisms often
voiced is that the word 'close' relates to the end of something,
whereas getting a sale from a customer should be the 'start' of a
relationship. Others feel it is too harsh a word and reflects badly
on their professionalism. Well I say 'phooey'!

I remember very well when I was given my first ever business
cards. I was so very proud to have them and sat and admired
them for some time. It had the name and address of my
company, my name, and underneath my name the single word
'Sales'. A few years later, whilst working with another company,
my title was changed and my card bore the title Sales Executive.
With the benefit of hindsight, it is quite obvious why the
company changed my title. It gave me more prestige (not more
money) and therefore made me feel better about myself. It also
made the potential customer feel they were dealing with
someone more important – an executive rather than a salesman.
A few years later, and around the time that consultative selling

became more fashionable, it became the norm for the title 'Sales Executive' to be replaced with 'Sales Consultant' and soon after that the word sales was dropped by many companies. In my case I became a Financial Consultant. In my opinion, the moment the word 'consultant' was introduced into the salesperson's title was the moment the rot set in! Salespeople stopped selling and became consultants and, as you well know, salespeople do not get paid for consulting; we get paid for selling.

The term 'close the sale' is brief, to the point, and we all know what it means. It means getting an order or getting an agreement to move on to the next stage in the buying process. Selling is the oldest profession and the term 'close the sale' has been used for hundreds of years and will probably be used for many hundreds more to come.

" selling is the oldest profession "

Death of the 'hard sell'

The days of the 'hard sell' are over for most companies and their sales team. The old 'foot in the door' approach rarely works any more. As I have previously stated, I believe totally in the concept of consultative selling. I believe that we must be focused on exploring our customers' needs and doing the very best for them we can. I believe that we must act with absolute honesty and integrity and that we must strive to build excellent and ongoing relationships with our customers and become their trusted adviser in our expert field. However, I also believe it is critical to our success that we never forget that we are selling, and it is my opinion that the hard sell just needs to be a lot more subtle and professional than it used to be. Here is an example to illustrate this point.

case study

The subtle approach

A client of mine recently asked me if I could recommend a marketing consultant who could assist him on a short-term, six-month contract to develop a marketing campaign for a new product range he was launching. I believed I knew the right person and set up a meeting with the three of us so that I could introduce my client to Jonathan. The important point to remember here is that my client hates to be sold to. I have seen him go into a frenzy at the slightest hint that somebody is trying to sell to him; it is not a pleasant sight and not a pleasant experience for the salesperson either. I also knew that Jonathan wanted this potentially very highly paid contract and, based on how I had seen him present himself in the past, I knew he was going to really sell himself to my client. It was going to be a very interesting meeting.

The three of us met a few days later. My client briefly outlined the project to Jonathan and then Jonathan took over. The meeting lasted 90 minutes and during that time I counted Jonathan asking 39 subtle, well worded, closing questions that my client responded to every time. Not once did my client realise he was being closed on giving Jonathan the contract, step-by-step throughout the presentation. When Jonathan left, my client asked, 'Well Bruce, what do you think?' 'What do *you* think?', I replied. He said, 'It's good to meet with someone who's not in the least pushy, is very professional and can obviously do the job. So if you are in agreement, I'm going to hire him.' The hard sell *is* indeed just a lot more subtle now!

If you don't ask for the order – you may not get it

Salespeople don't plan to fail but they often fail to close. This point was vividly illustrated to me some years ago by a shower salesman. My family and I had just moved to a very expensive neighbourhood. We had chosen a slightly smaller house than we really needed because of the high prices in the area and we decided to install a shower-room to ease the morning queue outside the bathroom.

A representative from a well-known company visited us late one afternoon. He was very presentable and knew his product well. I was impressed. He spent the first half an hour running through the various models that were available and the technical specifications of each. I mentally decided on the most appropriate one for our needs. After a tour of inspection of the house, and taking measurements in various rooms, the most appropriate site in which to install the equipment soon became very apparent. Over a cup of coffee we ran through the technical specifications of the model I had already set my mind on and the costs of supply, delivery and installation. I was ready to sign the order. At this point, the super-salesman thanked us for our time and patience, placed a quotation and some literature on our coffee-table, and got up and left. His parting words were, 'I'll wait to hear from you then.'

I was totally flabbergasted. I wanted the equipment. I wanted to buy it from his company and I was ready to sign an order form immediately, but he did not ask me to. His lack of enthusiasm or his fear of closing the sale rubbed off on me. The following day over breakfast my wife and I decided that we could probably do without the equipment anyway as it was very likely that we would be moving on again in a year or so.

You may think this is an extreme example but I can assure you that thousands of times every day, in every country throughout the world, a salesperson fails to ask for the order. Even when there is an obviously willing buyer and where the sale is there for the asking, the same rule applies. If you don't ask for it – you probably won't get it! Customers need help in making a buying decision. They find it hard to ask to buy and it is your responsibility to make it as easy as possible for them to do so.

“ customers need help in making a buying decision ”

In spite of that, the thought of closing the sale still seems to strike such terror into the hearts and minds of even the most experienced and competent salespeople. If it is the right prospect with the need and the means to buy, if the presentation has run smoothly and objections, if any, have been handled successfully, asking for the order should be the natural and obvious next step. So often it just does not happen. The target you have set for yourself is to double you sales – fast! If you do not ask for the business during and at the end of your presentation you are not going to achieve that, so I am going to share 10 of the best closing techniques that I know.

10 of the best closing techniques

The fact is that at least 90 per cent of the time when I am selling I only use numbers 1, 6 and 10 of the following, and you could do the same. So why have I included seven others?

There are two reasons for giving you these 10 closes. Firstly, they all work very well in many situations and it is good for you to know them all, even if you choose not to use them. The other reason is based on the fact that if we believe something will work for us, then it will, and if we believe something will not work for us, then it will not.

You may read through and study these 10 closes and believe that others will work better for you than the three I use most frequently. If that is the case, use those because you are right!

1 Get the prospect to close the sale

This close is the easiest, the least stressful to both the salesperson and the prospect, and if you only used this close, you would double your sales. Here is what you say after you have exposed all the pain you can and presented the features and benefits of your product or service and how they can solve the pain.

You: John, are you now 100 per cent certain that what I have to offer can solve those problems?

Prospect: *Yes.*

You: In that case, what would you like me to do now? (silent close). *Or* So what happens next? (silent close).

You have taken all the pressure off yourself but you have not put any pressure on the prospect. You have not asked them for the business; you have given them a choice. Of course the only sensible choice they can make is to go ahead and place an order with you.

2 Asking for the money

Getting an agreement on the pricing is another method for closing a sale. Now I know that many salespeople do not like asking for money, or even talking about money, and when the time comes the salesperson begins to get a little panicky and the easy flow of the presentation starts to stall.

Providing you have exposed sufficient pain and the prospect seems eager to deal with it, why should you have a problem asking for the money? Your prospect certainly was not expecting the solution to come without a cost and opening up the discussion on it as early as possible can also enable a prompt close. Therefore you can simply say, 'The investment required to solve these problems is going to be in the region of (£XXX). Is that going to be OK with you?' (silent close). If they respond with a 'Yes', you have made a sale.

If you have a variety of solutions to their pain, each with a different price point, you could deal with the price in a number of ways. For example:

You: Do you have a budget available to solve these problems?

Prospect: *Yes.*

You: Would you mind sharing that with me in round numbers? (silent close).

Or

You: Do you have a budget available to solve these problems?

Prospect: *No.*

You: How are you planning to pay for the solution then? (silent close).

Prospect: Well how much is it going to cost me?

You: As you can imagine, there's a number of ways we could solve these problems. Some solutions run from between £5000 to £10,000, others from £11,000 to £19,000 and sometimes we'll tailor packages at £20,000 plus – which of those price brackets do you think you'd be looking to work in?

The most important point I want you to be aware of is that it is perfectly all right, and indeed essential, to discuss money. If you hesitate, your prospect's subconscious mind will pick up on this and they will inevitably put pressure on you to reduce the final price because they know you do not like to discuss money and that you will be likely to agree, just to get it over with.

3 Start with a close

Salespeople who attend my Master Classes often ask me when they should start closing. My answer is very simple. You are starting to close from the moment that you start to speak. When you ask for the business it is just your final closing question.

If you are selling a product or service which can be closed in just one sales call, you can shorten the entire procedure and reverse the normal sales process by starting with a close. For example:

Salesperson to a couple who have just walked in to a bed showroom (it could be any other type of showroom): 'Good afternoon. Have you come here to buy a bed today?'

Salesperson selling office supplies calling on a customer for the first time: 'Good morning Mr Smith. Have you invited me in to place a first order with us today?'

Asking a closing question right at the beginning of your conversation is a very powerful technique. When you ask that question, your prospect's subconscious mind is involved in the response and tells them that they do really want and have a need to purchase what you are selling.

4 Turning a question into a sale

This is another very powerful closing technique and there are frequent opportunities to use it during many sales presentations. How can you turn a question from a prospect into a close? Let us look at a few examples:

Prospect: Does it come in red?

Salesperson: *Would you like it in red?*

Prospect: Yes. [They have bought it.]

Prospect: Is there a diesel version?

Salesperson: *Would you like a diesel version?*

Prospect: Yes. [They have bought it.]

Prospect: Can I pay for this monthly?

Salesperson: *Would you like to pay for it monthly?*

Prospect: Yes. [They have bought it.]

Turning a question into a sale will work wonders for your closing ratios and, with practice, can be introduced many times into any sales presentation. It can also be repeated, depending upon the other questions you may be asked. For example:

Prospect: Is this model available in a diesel version?

Salesperson: *Would you like it in a diesel version?*

Prospect: Possibly. Would it be available by the end of next week?

Salesperson: *If I can get it to you by then, can you approve the order today?*

Prospect: Yes. [They've bought it.]

5 The (invented) deadline close

The invented deadline close does not necessarily have to be invented and, in fact, I prefer that you did not invent one. I firmly believe that acting without integrity attracts people who will act without integrity with you. Nevertheless, I mention it because it is used frequently by many companies to encourage people swiftly to sign on the dotted line. There will, however, often be times when you have a limited number of end-of-range products, or when you are offering a discount on a product or service because your company is going through a particularly quiet patch.

The financial services industry is fortunate in respect of genuine deadlines. Frequent changes in taxation and legislation and anticipated changes prior to the announcement of the government's Budget strategy, gives financial services salespeople countless opportunities to present prospects or clients with dead-lines that could provide opportunities to save, or make money if they act quickly.

Here are some examples of deadline closes that have been presented to me. I have no idea if they were invented or genuine.

Example 1

Mr King, we currently have a CRM program which is being used by some of the major corporations in the country. These have been installed only quite recently and, according to our information, will be satisfactory for these very companies for at least 10 to 15 years. However, we recently hired a team of programmers to develop a new system for us which, frankly, I do not believe is a good decision by our CEO. The costs of this new CRM program are likely to be at least 30 per cent more than that of our existing version. We can only offer the current one for another 30 days and have limited capacity to supervise the installation, so if you are looking to save a considerable sum of money, I'd suggest you invest in this system right now.

Example 2

Mr King, I have inside information from the sales department at the manufacturers that this model is soon to be replaced by the updated version, which is going to cost some £5000 more. I also happen to know that the increased cost is not justified as the improvements are minor. However, we will be committed to taking this stock, as will all other dealers, and we are therefore prepared to offer you one of the last few of this model, and with an additional 5 per cent discount.

This type of close is nothing more than a sophisticated version of the 'last one' close used by so many retailers. Probably the classic example of this is when my wife is being sold a very expensive dress or coat in a store. If she is showing more than the slightest interest the salesperson will probably say: 'Before you get too enthusiastic about this particular style Mrs King, I had better check in the storeroom and see if we have your size. This is a very limited edition and has been very popular.' Of course, she returns a few minutes later with the information that there is only one left. My wife usually buys it, although I suspect there is usually a whole rack of her size in the storeroom. Of course, I've never told her that.

6 The secondary question close

Use this close when you are fairly certain that your prospect is willing to accept your proposition and all that is necessary is to put it to bed quickly. The technique is based on posing the major buying question first, then immediately by-passing it with another question of lesser importance which is much easier to make a decision on than the main purchase. Here are a few examples:

You: I think we have covered everything to your satisfaction now Mr Prospect. We just need to complete the order form. By the way, will you be arranging your own insurance, or would you like us to arrange this for you?

Prospect: *I will be arranging my own insurance, thank you.* [They've bought it.]

You: From what we have discussed so far Mr Prospect, I think the computer with 1000 gigabytes is going to be most suitable for you. Would you prefer it with a black or silver case?

Prospect: *I would prefer black.* [They've bought it.]

You: From what we've discussed, the Bahamas seems to be the ideal holiday for you and your family. Will you be paying by cheque or credit card?

Prospect: *By credit card.* [They've bought it.]

The psychology behind this type of close is very simple. As I stated previously, it is the salesperson's responsibility to make the close as easy and painless for the prospect as possible. Giving them the opportunity to agree to some very minor point means that the major decision, and the most expensive one, is taken out of the picture completely. Buyer resistance vanishes with this close.

7 The weak spot close

Some years ago I was involved with a house-building company in Scotland. We had built a number of small, luxury holiday homes on a lake-shore site. They had the most magnificent views but, due to cost constraints, the rooms had been kept to a minimal size and we had not been able to use the highest standards of fixtures and fittings as we would have wished. Nevertheless, the homes were selling reasonably well, although not nearly as fast as we had hoped.

One bright afternoon I was showing prospective purchasers around the development and was keen to sell the house in which this couple had expressed some slight interest. It was one of the first to be built and had been on our hands a long time.

The very first thing the wife said when she walked into the kitchen was: 'Oh, what a wonderful view. I was brought up in a home overlooking a lake and I have always wanted to live somewhere like this again.' This was her 'weak spot'. We then moved into the living-room. The husband expressed concern at its dimensions. I immediately pointed out the open fireplace and the wonderful view across the lake. We then moved upstairs into the first bedroom. The same sequence of events took place there and in the other two bedrooms. In each case the husband expressed concern at the size of the rooms and also commented on the quality of the fixtures and fittings. I agreed, and pointed out the wonderful view across the lake from each bedroom.

Although I was talking to the husband most of the time, I was really selling to the wife. It came as no surprise to me that, after a few minutes by themselves in their car, they returned and made me an offer. I refused this and stuck out for the full asking price. 'Is there anywhere else with a view across a lake quite like this?' I asked. They bought the house at the full market price.

❝ look out for a prospect's weak spots ❞

Look out for a prospect's weak spots. They occur in almost every type of market and with almost every type of buyer. Whenever an objection is raised, acknowledge it and then remind your prospect of that single feature that is so very attractive to them.

8 The take it home and try it close

This close almost never fails with the right product or service and I believe the first person to use this technique was a pet shop owner in California. He used to get so many people visiting his pet shop who loved looking at the puppies and playing with them, but only a small percentage ever bought them. Then he came up with a cunning plan.

As soon as a parent with children came into the store and started looking at the puppies, he would approach them and say, 'Sir (or Madam), you really shouldn't even think about buying a puppy today. Sometimes they get on famously with a new owner and sometimes it can be a real disaster. Sometimes they get on great with kids like yours and sometimes they don't. Tell you what I'll do though. I'll let you take this little fellow home for a few days and you can see if he fits in and gets on with everybody. If he doesn't, you just bring him back. Would you like to do that?'

The kids would scream 'Mummy, Mummy – can we do that please!' and Mummy (or Daddy) could hardly ever say no. Neither did many puppies ever come back.

The same technique has been used to sell automobiles, televisions and other electronic products, paintings and a host of other goods in both the consumer and business market.

9 The blank order form close

Many products or services require an order form or authority for your prospect to sign. If you do not have one, maybe you could design one.

Without making it too obvious, try to make sure that your order form is in front of you, and in view of your prospect, either at the start of your presentation or some time during it when you produce reference literature or testimonials. At some stage, when you feel your prospect is ready to be closed, ask for a piece of information that you require to fulfil their order and write it on the form. It could be your prospect's full name, their company's name or address, or information relating to one of the products or services you are selling.

The moment your prospect sees you write something on your blank order form and does not question it, you know they have bought. The rest of the sales process is usually a mere formality.

In some sales situations it can be appropriate to enter the company's name and address on the form even before you get into the meeting. By leaving this in full view of your prospect, with their name and address at the top in bold capital letters, you are sending a very clear message to their subconscious mind that you expect a sale.

10 The doorknob close

I have used the doorknob close throughout my selling career and I estimate that it has increased my sales by at least 10 to 15 per cent over that time. That equates to a lot of money.

You use the doorknob close when you have tried everything you can possibly do to make a sale and there is nothing left but to quit.

You pack your briefcase, rise from your chair, thank your prospect warmly for seeing you and giving you the opportunity to demonstrate your product or service to them. As you get to the door, you push or pull it half open, and keeping your hand on the doorknob, you half turn around and make the following statement:

You: Mr Prospect, just before I go, may I please take my sales hat off and ask you one more question?'

Prospect: OK then.

You: I hope you don't mind me asking but, as I am sure you are aware, I make my living selling this particular product. I thought I had presented it to you properly. I felt you had the need for it and that I had demonstrated the benefits to you accurately. I was quite certain that you would want to invest in it. Just so that I don't make the same mistake again, could you please tell me where I went wrong?

The door is still half open, your prospect thinks you are leaving and they are therefore off the hook and relaxed. With your salesperson's hat off, they are even sympathetic and eager to help. They finally give you the real reason. Then it is up to you to get back in the chair and deal with that final objection. It takes a little bit of nerve, but it is worth the effort.

Closing the sale after a good presentation has never been difficult. Using these closing techniques should make it a lot easier for you.

Key action points

■ It is your responsibility to make it easy for your prospect to make the purchase by asking them for the business – closing the sale.

■ Study the 10 closes and select just a few that you believe will be the most useful to you, learn them and put them into practice.

■ Continue with the *GAVA double your sales – fast* process daily.

■ Please study and work on applying the techniques in this Master Class for at least one week.

Final words

You are possibly familiar with the following statistics:

- We remember 5 per cent of what we *hear*.
- We remember 20 per cent of what we *see*.
- We remember 50 per cent of what we *do*.

If you have been following this programme as I recommended, you will have been *doing* what I have taught you in these Master Classes and you will have either doubled your sales or are well on your way to achieving that.

You are possibly less familiar with the fact that we remember 90 per cent or more of what we *teach*!

I've taught the material in this programme to tens of thousands of salespeople around the world, which is why I'm considered such an expert at selling. Now it is your turn. If you are a sales manager, teach these Master Classes to your sales team. If you are a salesperson, teach and share this information with your colleagues. By doing so, you too will remember more and you could go on to double your sales again – and again.

My warmest wishes

Bruce King

P.S. Do sign up for my free newsletter at www.bruceking.co.uk and I'll keep you regularly updated with tips and strategies to help you to sell even more.

Index